Words
That Make
Pictures

Creative Journalism in the Digital Age

Eating for 14 hours at a stretch, an elephant consumes over three tons of food a day – and if still hungry will eat wood from whole branches wrenched from trees

While elephants hunted for their tusks are in danger of extinction in other parts of Africa, Botswana's ruthless policy of shooting ivory poachers on sight is creating a very different problem

GENTLE GIANTS
or
RAMPAGING
MONSTERS?

Desperate measures may be needed to control the numbers of a creature seemingly capable of heart-rending grief at the loss of its baby and yet capable of wreaking mass destruction on an entire environment

The kill was before first light. The funeral took place that afternoon. A lioness, returning empty-bellied from a nocturnal prowl in Botswana's Chobe National Park, spotted a baby elephant separated from its herd in the night and walking uncertainly along a shallow valley.

Her muzzle and pale stomach only inches from the ground, her tawny coat almost invisible in the grey gloom, the lioness made its feline stalk to within 15 metres downwind of its prey – then exploded into a rush and pounce. Claws sank into the elephant's neck, pulling it to the ground, jaws tearing open the exposed throat. The baby elephant would have died without a whimper.

Over the next two hours, the lioness enjoyed a leisurely breakfast, watched by her three cubs hidden in a grove of the woolly caper bush overlooking the valley. Only when she exchanged places with them, allowing three smaller mouths to explore the crimson tunnel she had made into the carcass, was there activity from the surrounding trees.

All morning a growing assembly of vultures had flown into view, lining every bough, necks sunken, eyes fixed on the small mountain of flesh. Now they took to the air and paraglided into a semi-circle around the dead elephant, landing gaitered feet first, wings unfurled to the span of a boastful fisherman, then promptly folded tight as an umbrella.

Undeterred, the cubs continued tearing out flesh from within the armoured hide. They

Bold images pull readers into the page but then the words need to create pictures of their own to hold their attention

Words That Make Pictures

Creative Journalism in the Digital Age

By Peter Grayling Jackson

The Crowood Press

For Charles Stainsby,
the editor who set me free

First published in 2018 by
The Crowood Press Ltd
Ramsbury, Marlborough
Wiltshire SN8 2HR

www.crowood.com

© Peter Grayling Jackson 2018

British Library Cataloguing-in-Publication Data
A catalogue record for this book is available from the British Library.

ISBN 978 1 78500 459 9

Designed by Clive Crook and Janet McCallum

Printed and bound in India by Parksons Graphics

Contents

Preface

This book stems from thirty years' experience as a writer, commissioning editor and publisher together with a decade as a lecturer in multimedia journalism.

It was then that I formalized the four principal ingredients of successful deployment of the written word in this digital age and it was there that each autumn's intake of freshers complained of a return to the kindergarten in being handed red, blue, green and black felt-tip pens and required to colour-code those four vital elements in the published features we chose to examine.

That first physical act of applying the coloured pens to paper was to emphasize the need to pick out the differing roles played by each paragraph and to see how they each contributed to the overall effect.

The students quickly became aware that this initial process provided a striking visual analysis of the strengths and weaknesses of a feature, and in subsequent exercises were required to mentally position four distinctive symbols – we called them our 'hallmarks' – throughout a piece to identify how a well-balanced pattern of those four elements constituted an absorbing piece of writing.

Multimedia students are taught that journalism is a basic craft and that the digital age has provided a series of platforms from which to engage the reader. So they learn to service websites and all forms of social media that add the dimensions of sound, moving pictures and a sense of interactivity to the written word.

It seemed to me that if words being assembled at any length (on page or on screen) were to retain their hold on the reader, the writer must make a special effort to break free from the impression of solid columns of words and match the vitality of the new dimensions.

Knowing my students were becoming accomplished in video and audio production (as is increasingly required in all forms of contemporary journalism), I encouraged them to approach the construction of a feature with the mind of a broadcaster – thinking how a TV director might set his opening scene with a stunning zoom lens close-up or a piece of vivid video, getting the central character to deliver a powerful quote into camera, capturing relevant background noises.

Hence, the need for words fashioned in a form that leaps from the page or screen in a way to convince the reader that they are looking in on animated action rather than the eye merely following serried ranks of type, that they are absorbing information through a sense of being able to witness what exactly is going on.

Hence, the need for **Words That Make Pictures**.

Acknowledgments

I am indebted to the journalists whose work was analyzed by students at Bournemouth University's Media School over the period of more than a decade. Not only were these fine examples of the writer's craft an invaluable teaching aid, they inspired our graduates to go out into the world of media with the loftiest of ambitions.   PGJ

In the Beginning ...

The annual conference of the magazine publishing industry for 2014 had 'reinvention' as its theme and there was lots of talk about 'burning platforms', 'brand journeys', 'native advertising' and 'monetizing touchpoints'.

All good stuff but for me three things stood out:

- DC Thomson CEO Ellis Watson exhorting 'journalists and publishers to get out there and deliver exciting and compelling content'.
- Sarah Bailey, editor-in-chief of *Red* magazine, wanting to remind her readers of the 'deep pleasure of reading'.
- Ellis, again, warning publishers not to 'burn the floorboards to keep warm'. Editorial budgets must be protected.

Because, when all is said and done, quality content, specifically written quality content, is what it's all about, and it doesn't matter a jot whether you're reading it in print, on a tablet, a smartphone or the back of a cereal packet.

Video has a great place in our future, as does, to a lesser extent, audio, but well-written WORDS will always be our trump card, distinguishing professional publishers from the rest.

Look at your own reading habits. In the magazines and newspapers you read, there will be certain writers you always look out for. Take them out of the equation and your loyalty to that particular title can no longer be taken for granted.

Great writers are why we purchase newspapers and magazines in the first place. Insightful, compelling, humorous, affecting, authoritative, wise, thought-provoking – their facility with words can be breathtaking.

Of course, not all content is equal and that is why the 'quality' prefix is so important. Take two 1600-word pieces by two different writers. About the only thing you can say with certainty is they occupy the same amount of publishing estate. Everything else, the important stuff, comes from within the mind of the author. Beware producing content for content's sake. Produce Ellis Watson's 'exciting and compelling content', otherwise probably best not to bother.

But great writers are a scarce commodity. They don't grow on trees. Proficiency can be taught, but not brilliance. The best ones will have innate curiosity, strong passions and deep interests, and will in all likelihood have been voracious readers and prolific writers from an early age. The advice to would-journalists from Tony Parsons (newspaperman turned best-selling novelist) no doubt mirrors his own experience: 'Read, read, read, write, write, write'.

Great writers are valuable and need to be nurtured. Your editorial policy will dictate your future success. Build a great stable of writers and you will reap the reward. Slash, skimp and salami-slice your editorial budget and you will starve your title of life-giving oxygen.

If technology is your primary focus then you will end up with a great platform populated with sub-standard content and … no subscribers.

Ellis Watson describes publishers' obsession with technology as 'getting ridiculous'. Emap's Natasha Christie-Miller relates how on taking over Emap she found the company 'distracted' by technology. The company had lost sight of what was important, namely, content.

Don't get me wrong. A deep awareness of how your readers want to read your content is crucially important, but when you are next drawing up your budget stop and think – what is it that makes your title special?

… it's the words, stupid "

JAMES EVELEGH, Editor, *InPublishing* magazine

Standing on the cliff-top overlooking  white-walled cottages of a Cornish fishing village, Andrew Durham shakes his ____ en surveying the surfers happily riding the rolling Atlantic breakers down below.

Forty-seven-year-old Durham, a jaunt__ __re in a faded duffel coat and scarlet baseball cap, is coxswain of the Pendurest life____ __ore than 350 stationed around the British Isles – all solely maintained by volunt___ __nations.

'In summer these waters are a holidaymaker's paradise,' he says, speaking above the squeals of circling seagulls. 'But com____ __, when the great sou-westers start blowing in, you're looking at the most treach____ __as in the world.'

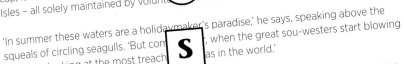

Last month he was called from his bed at 3am and rode his bicycle through the night to join his crewmates in launching their lifeboat and setting off through mountainous seas to reach a German freighter that had run on to rocks. Survivors scrambling to safety down the side of the steeply listing shi__ __orted that the skipper was refusing to leave. 'I had to climb on board and found____ __ched in a corner of the bridge, cradling his pet Alsatian dog,' Durham recalls. 'He spoke little English but managed to convey that he could not leave with the dog because he understood it would be taken from him if he landed in Britain because of quarantine regulations. I managed to convince him that it would be better if they both lived and I got them on the lifeboat before the freighter finally broke up.'

Words That Make Pictures seeks to establish a formula for identifying the four principal ingredients of successful deployment of words in this digital age

1 Why Words Need to Make Pictures

Competing with the all-encompassing imagery of the web, the writer must utilize all the tools of non-fiction to gain the most impact from reality

Journalism has never been more vibrant. Set free from the limitations of mere words on paper, the multimedia journalist is a packager of video, audio, graphics and archive film. The screen may be static but within it people, situations and destinations are brought to life before the eyes of the countless million inhabitants of the digital world.

Yet there is still a place for print. Still a demand for writers of the longer-read features of journals of analysis and opinion, of weekend newspapers and their many supplements and of magazines of every sort. Still a bright career for the journalist who can capture mood and atmosphere, turn a memorable phrase, coin an evocative headline.

But he must be aware of the special opposition brought about by the digital revolution.

World of utter belief

If seeing is supposedly believing, we live in a world of utter belief because everything is made visible for us.

Telephones, which once merely carried voices along wires, now enable us to look upon the caller. Where radio was sounds coming through a loudspeaker we can now peer into the studio by way of a webcam. The gramophone record progressed to the LP that became the CD that has become DVD, which means we can watch the artistes perform. Television's zoom lens takes the couch-bound rugby fan into the heart of a scrum 10,000 miles away; the Hawkeye device enables the cricket follower to look through the body of the batsman and see if the ball would have hit the stumps. Medical scanners can portray every part of our physique and enable us to witness the very beginnings of human life within the womb. And man has ventured into space and beamed back pictures of Mother Earth itself – that blue/grey orb floating in a blackness of eternity that poets have spent centuries trying to describe in imagination.

So what of mere words?

This book is an affirmation of the rich and exciting future of the word whether appearing on paper or transferred to the smartphone, tablet or laptop in our increasingly digitized world. The challenge is

We can now witness the very beginnings of human life within the womb and look down on Mother Earth from outer space

The book is safe. Physical sales are boosted by cut-price retailers operating online and many, many millions more are downloaded digitally

for the frozen word to find the way to match the urgency and impact of these riches of animated images.

News stories can be flashed around the globe, reaching the screens of billions of those smartphones, tablets and laptops in an electronic instant. The world-wide web offers immediate access to a monstrous library of information on almost every topic known to man, which persuades many screen-gazers to posit the inevitable demise of those venerable descendants of the Gutenberg revolution – the book, the newspaper and the magazine.

The book is safe. Indeed, more physical books are being sold than ever, not least brought to the door through online cut-price retailers. Many, many millions more books are increasingly downloaded digitally – especially formerly paperback novels of the type taken as holiday reading and left behind on the beach. But a digital book is something as seen through a window; it has no substance, it is leased rather than possessed, it presupposes a home without a bookshelf. So publishers will be seeking to improve the quality of paper, enriching the level of illustration, enhancing the texture of the binding to cater for the still massive audience that cherishes ownership of the words they enjoy. But whether digital or in print, a book's a book for all that and will certainly survive.

Newspapers have embraced the enemy

News is now a 24-hour commodity. No matter how fast the presses, no matter how slick the distribution, the paper arriving at the breakfast table is delivering yesterday's news. It limps sadly behind TV, radio and online sources which promise 'news as it happens'.

But that does not mean the death of newspapers. Most have embraced the enemy in developing their own websites which not only provide instant updates but add the elements of sound and moving pictures to their menu. Hard copy sales have inevitably declined but overall readership has soared by way of access to a vast electronic audience. And the newsprint editions have become more magazine-like, concentrating on features, analysis and opinion.

So if newspapers are turning into magazines to survive what does the future hold for magazines themselves?

They, too, produce their online versions – often with more effective results than newspapers because magazines have much more sharply focused audiences. They do not have to offer all things to everyone. Successful magazines develop a family affinity with their readers and

Hard copy sales of newspapers have inevitably declined but overall readership has soared by way of access to a vast electronic audience

are thus in a position to target them accordingly.

A newspaper is a window on the world and the view through the window can change every day – portraying disasters, scandals, political drama, financial crises, international tensions. The agenda is beyond its control.

When, for example, a regular reader of a woman's magazine turns the cover she opens the door to a familiar room full of people she knows and who know her. For a man and his favourite title, it's the sensation of entering a club of kindred spirits. Everything is relevant, the agenda is fixed. And for many, the actual purchase and possession of a hard copy remains a statement of commitment to that club membership.

Sacred trilogy

Thus totally aware of their specific readership, magazine features pursue their own sacred trilogy:

To inform (what specially concerns your business or profession, what's going on within your personal lifestyle – what's new in cars and travel and fashion; what's the latest in the arts and show business);

To educate (how to further your career, how to invest, how to slim, how to cook, how to play golf, how to do-it-yourself); and

To entertain (providing content that is enjoyable to read, presented within a package intended to be a pleasure to possess).

Big, big difference

ENTERTAINMENT – That is a big, big difference between the vast majority of words appearing online and words comprising the feature pages of magazines.

Information and Education abound within the world of Googling but how many people go there to be Entertained? Chasing a mouse across its pad, endlessly flicking a touch screen, is not consciously the most pleasurable of experiences. But the screen, whether small or larger, delivers all that is asked of it with incredible efficiency..

By comparison with the tactile experience of curling up with a magazine (and from now on this term includes the feature elements

Magazines seek to engender a sense of club membership and for many the actual purchase and possession of a hard copy remains a statement of commitment to that club

Stemming from the BBC's founding philosophy of seeking to Inform, Educate and Entertain, magazines have embraced the same mission as their sacred trilogy

Dramatic magazine covers can attract thousands of extra customers but research shows it's pictures which pull them into the stories inside and persuade them to start reading

of newspapers), using the world-wide web has been compared to ordering dinner from a hotel's room service instead of eating in the restaurant. One can be seen as a purely functional activity which promptly delivers the required food and drink for private consumption in an anonymous bedroom; the other can be a memorable social and gastronomic experience in an animated setting.

Defined as 'an illustrated periodical', the magazine understands the power of pictures. The potency of a cover image on a crowded newsstand can add tens of thousands of copies to the circulation. Research shows that it's pictures which pull would-be purchasers into individual pages when they turn inside.

But it's only the accompanying words which can arrest that interest and turn browsers into readers. It's only when a magazine is read that it becomes alive, not merely a glossy wad of newsprint. And there is a way to ensure that those words can remain very much alive when they are increasingly transposed to a screen.

Reading from the screen is slower

Online sites offer words by the million to go with their all-dancing, all-singing video and audio elements. But any writing specifically aimed at the small screen tends to be essentially economical in style if extravagant in availability. It is established that because text on screen has much less resolution than ink on paper people read 25 per cent more slowly online and find it harder to retain information. The result is a preference for short, sharp sentences and slim-line paragraphs anticipating the brief attention span of web surfers, often idly passing by, or information junkies seeking a quick fix. For them, it has little more passion than an old Yellow Pages directory. The blunt offer is: You want it; We got it; You come and find it.

But if people will happily read 100,000 words of uninterrupted text in a novel brought to a digital tablet on their lap there is no way a well-crafted magazine feature of up to 2,000 words cannot transfer to the screen.

The novel is easily digestible because novelists paint pictures in words of their characters, situations, landscapes, emotions; the telling of even the heaviest drama is meant to be **enjoyed**.

Gay Talese, one of America's greatest magazine writers, used all of those devices in producing what he termed 'non-fiction about real people' – drenching his observations with colourful detail

In 'Frank Sinatra has a cold,' one of his most famous pieces for

Because text on screen has much less resolution than ink on paper people read 25 per cent more slowly online and find it harder to retain information

Esquire magazine, he described how Sinatra had even the soles of his shoes polished and that he was followed everywhere by a grey-haired lady with a selection of toupees – 'holding his hair in a tiny satchel'.

A feature writer adopting the non-fiction approach to reality can go far beyond mere reportage.

Thus:

'Charles Wilson, a 57-year-old bank manager' becomes 'Bank manager Charles Wilson wore middle age like a proud uniform, from the burnished dome of his bald head to the glazed toecaps of his sturdy shoes via a waistcoat puffed with self-importance...'

'Henrietta Thompson, of 21, Dormer Avenue, Kingsbury' becomes 'Henrietta's suburban home was a flaking pebble-dashed bungalow which regarded the world through sullen lace-curtained windows, the front lawn long surrendered to a celebration of crazy paving...'

One version is fact, the other a picture.

> The non-fiction approach to feature writing can fire the imagination of the reader by turning mere reportage into Words That Make Pictures

Competing with the screen

In this way, the feature can hold its audience by seeking to beguile – by tempting the reader into the heart of stories which fire the imagination in a way that more than competes with the Web's relentless weight of information, by striving to deploy Words That Make Pictures

Which is why good writing now needs to be more than relevant facts assembled within a neatly arranged sequence of words. Those words must be deliberately deployed to conjure up images which enable the reader to look in on the characters within the setting of their story, to hear them talking, to inhabit their feelings.

The test to be made after every written passage is: Have I enabled the reader to see, to hear and to feel? Of course, the best writing was ever thus.

Caitlin Moran, award-winning columnist for *The Times* and a best-selling author, likens the role of the writer as supplying images to what she terms the 'projection screen' within the reader's mind.

Addressing the reader, she writes: 'If I type "dragon" – casually, just six letters, no effort for me – suddenly, a dragon appears in your mind. You have to make it. Your brain fires up – perhaps your heartbeat will speed a little, depending on if you have had previous unhappy experiences with dragons. Perhaps you will have given her golden claws – or maybe you have a fondness for tight, black shiny scales. But however closely I have described her, she will still be your dragon – in

> Words must be deliberately deployed to conjure up vivid images which enable the reader to look in on the character within the setting of their story, to hear them talking, to inhabit their emotions

The multimedia journalist must always work with two screens in view – one in the reader's mind, the other online

your head ... And no one else will ever see her.'

Which is why we are invariably disappointed on leaving a cinema showing the movie of a favourite book.

Because if it had caught our imagination we had already filmed the book in our own minds, cast the characters, inhabited their space, recorded the soundtrack. Hollywood often breaks the spell.

Difficulty in identifying

Who could identify the gangling, all-American Nicolas Cage with the sentimental Italian hero of *Captain Corelli's Mandolin*? Or the boyishly elegant David Hemmings with the caddish bravado of Flashman? Or an upholstered Albert Finney wearing a jokeshop moustache as the dapper Hercules Poirot? Or the chocolate TV commercial male model George Lazenby as James Bond. Or Mick Jagger hiding under a saucepan helmet as Australia's fearless Ned Kelly?

Most great novelists never had the cinema screen in mind; the royalties from a film-of-the-book came as a pleasant bonus for their success in creating such convincing images.

But the modern journalist must always deliberately write with screens in mind – that projection screen within the reader's mind and the myriad digital screens which are competing for that reader's attention.

Only by words that make pictures can writing that sets out to **Entertain** as well as to Inform and to Educate expect to survive in this visual world.

Fashioned with that in view, good writing can only triumph and endure.

2 Your Hallmarks of Excellence

The single page of copy below contains the four basic elements required to assemble **Words That Make Pictures**. Assemble is the word because feature writing is essentially a work of construction

Standing on the cliff-top overlooking the white-walled cottages of a Cornish fishing village, Andrew Durham shakes his head when surveying the surfers happily riding the rolling Atlantic breakers down below.

Forty-seven-year-old Durham, a jaunty figure in a faded duffel coat and scarlet baseball cap, is coxswain of the Pendurest lifeboat, one of more than 350 stationed around the British Isles – all solely maintained by voluntary donations.

'In summer these waters are a holidaymaker's paradise,' he says, speaking above the squeals of circling seagulls. 'But come winter, when the great sou-westers start blowing in, you're looking at the most treacherous seas in the world.'

Last month he was called from his bed at 3am and rode his bicycle through the night to join his crewmates in launching their lifeboat and setting off through mountainous seas to reach a German freighter that had run on to rocks. Survivors scrambling to safety down the side of the steeply listing ship reported that the skipper was refusing to leave.

'I had to climb on board and found him crouched in a corner of the bridge, cradling his pet Alsatian dog,' Durham recalls. 'He spoke little English but managed to convey that he could not leave with the dog because he understood it would be taken from him if he landed in Britain because of quarantine regulations. I managed to convince him that it would be better if they both lived and I got them on the lifeboat before the freighter finally broke up.'

Multimedia journalism revels in a sense of urgency. Breaking stories online are often hastily assembled with whatever elements first come to hand, then progressively augmented, refined and restructured to produce a polished package.

News journalism was ever thus because the reporting of news is a reactive process – the recording of events as they unfold.

Traditional newspaper practice is for the the essence of the story to be contained in the opening paragraph, amplified by a series of statements which follow in order of significance. This enables the sub-editor to make any necessary cuts from the bottom up so ensuring that the story can be trimmed to the available space with the loss of only the least important parts. The last paragraph is the first to go.

News online works to a similar pattern when presenting on screen but to an extreme degree in that the first sentence in each descending paragraph should flag up the main point of its content and seek to provide links that signpost the extra dimensions that multimedia can display.

A fully rounded story online will encompass four elements:

VISUALS – pictures of the relevant people and places

INFORMATION – facts conveyed by voice-over, scrolling text and graphics

SOUNDS – quotes from central characters and background noises

ACTION – live video and archive film

If news is reactive then feature journalism is proactive in that the writer most often originates the idea, is allocated a given word-count, conducts their own research and when assembling the final material has control of both the first and last paragraphs in devising a smooth flow from beginning to end. A conclusion which echoes the thrust of the introduction – a pay-off that complements the intro – gives a feature the taste of a satisfying sandwich, with the substance neatly contained. The last paragraph is as important as the first and often the most memorable.

Whereas the news journalist is constantly harried by a shortage of time (especially the online newsman working to a frenzy of rolling headlines around the clock), the diligent feature journalist will often end up collecting too much material in the time made available. This is where he must identify the various categories of ingredients he has

A feature with a pay-off line that complements the intro provides a satisfying sandwich, with the substance neatly contained

unearthed, trim them to achieve a reasonable balance overall and then position them within the piece to provide variation of tone and pace and texture. So let us find a way to make them easily identifiable.

It is the putting together of a feature or an online story which determines whether the content glows or flickers. And the ingredients that guarantee a successful feature in print are the same as online:

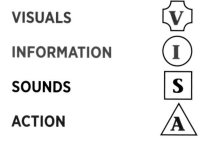

VISUALS

INFORMATION

SOUNDS

ACTION

These symbols are used to break down the four basic elements of the piece about the lifeboatman and illustrate how they fluently come together to produce Words That Make Pictures. Come to regard these symbols almost as a silversmith's hallmarks stamped upon the body of the text – and the right pattern of hallmarks is the stamp of excellence.

There is no suggestion that each must be given equal weight on all occasions. This will vary according to the subject matter and target publication, but with very few exceptions the best features will incorporate some proportion of each.

On the next page, we have a simple demonstration of how these 'hallmarks' can be put to work:

Standing on the cliff-top overlooking the white-walled cottages of a Cornish fishing village, Andrew Durham shakes his head when surveying the surfers happily riding the rolling Atlantic breakers down below.

Forty-seven-year-old Durham, a jaunty figure in a faded duffel coat and scarlet baseball cap, is coxswain of the Pendurest lifeboat, one of more than 350 stationed around the British Isles – all solely maintained by voluntary donations.

'In summer these waters are a holidaymaker's paradise,' he says, speaking above the squeals of circling seagulls. 'But come winter, when the great sou-westers start blowing in, you're looking at the most treacherous seas in the world.'

Last month he was called from his bed at 3am and rode his bicycle through the night to join his crewmates in launching their lifeboat and setting off through mountainous seas to reach a German freighter that had run on to rocks. Survivors scrambling to safety down the side of the steeply listing ship reported that the skipper was refusing to leave.

'I had to climb on board and found him crouched in a corner of the bridge, cradling his pet Alsatian dog,' Durham recalls. 'He spoke little English but managed to convey that he could not leave with the dog because he understood it would be taken from him if he landed in Britain because of quarantine regulations. I managed to convince him that it would be better if they both lived and I got them on the lifeboat before the freighter finally broke up.'

V The opening paragraph is of prime importance in providing **VISUALS**. It enables the reader to **see** Andrew Durham standing on the clifftop, to **see** the white-walled cottages, to **see** his face, to **see** the surfers, to **see** the Atlantic breakers.

I This paragraph contains that without which an article would be an empty sandwich – **INFORMATION**. Here in three lines are five hard facts – the man's age, his job, his employer, the number of lifeboat stations and their maintenance by voluntary donation.

In seeking to delight and surprise the readers, a feature must always be imparting interesting information so that they reach the conclusion of the piece with a murmur of satisfaction and the thought: 'Well, I never knew that.'

The editor of an American men's magazine would pose the following question after reading the first draft of a story submitted for publication: 'OK, but what's the takeaway?'

It was his way of questioning what the reader would get out of it, what would add to their knowledge, what would remain in their mind long after reading the piece.

The very best word-of-mouth recommendation of a publication is when a regular reader can impart some unusual piece of information to the man in the pub or a neighbour over the coffee table and prompt the question: 'But how on earth did you find that out?' The answer is simple – the title of the magazine or newspaper or website.

> The big question is 'But how on earth did you find that out?'

$\boxed{\text{S}}$ Since it's approaching a century since Hollywood made pictures talk this paragraph delivers that dimension of **SOUNDS**. Having been enabled to meet Durham, the reader wants to hear what he's got to say – above the shrieking of the seagulls.

Judith Woods, columnist for the *Daily Telegraph*, recalls her childhood in Northern Ireland during The Troubles as a series of Sounds:

> The crack of sniper fire, the clatter of Chinooks, the cavernous boom in the nights as the cinema was blown up yet again, followed, several beats later, by the plangent wail of sirens.

These paragraphs signify **ACTION**. Hollywood gave us the talkies but they were above all *movies*. So the Words That Make Pictures must ensure they deliver moving images.

Having learned what he does in $\textcircled{I}$ and heard him speak in $\boxed{\text{S}}$, the reader wants to see Durham in A This could be the writer providing an eye-witness account of the coxswain in the course of making an actual rescue or in this case describing a previous mission. The latter is an anecdote (which my dictionary defines as 'a short narrative of an incident') and anecdotes are the golden nuggets of feature writing because they bring facts, situations and traits of behaviour to life.

In its heyday, *Reader's Digest* used to instruct its writers thus: 'State it – Prove it'

If a rock musician is described as bad-tempered, give examples of

Anecdotes provide the writer with the chance to make a change of pace

him hurling a microphone from the stage or trashing a hotel bedroom. If a racing driver admits to being accident-prone reconstruct his most miraculous escape. If a playboy is known as a reckless gambler recreate the scene in the casino on the night he made his greatest loss. If a scientist wins a Nobel prize for a medical breakthrough let the reader share the events which led to his Eureka moment.

When the journalist turns playwright

In developing an anecdote, the journalist turns playwright in producing a mini-drama which is strong on atmosphere and heightens the elements of suspense and surprise. This invariably involves a change of pace within a feature, the close focus on a particular situation within the general flow of narrative. Above all, it represents a happening.

The anecdote of the German shipwreck would be represented by a clip of film should the piece on Andrew Durham constitute the first item of a storyboard for turning the story into an online documentary.

The setting within the **V** paragraphs would provide the **VISUALS** through a wide-angle shot of the scene, with the camera closing in to show the fishing village and the ocean in the background, then centring on the tiny figure on the cliff-top and finally moving to a close up of his face.

I indicating the basic **INFORMATION** would be provided by a voice-over or text scrolling across the bottom of the screen or a map of the area.

The **SOUNDS** described in the **S** paragraph would be delivered by Durham talking into camera – with those noisy birds providing an atmospheric background.

A would be delivering **ACTION** by way of an archive sequence taken from the RNLI video archives.

A student's simple storyboard for an online version of the lifeboatman story

Video longshot moving to close-up

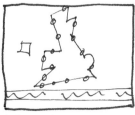

Information – map showing lifeboat stations in UK

Into camera quotes from lifeboatman

RNLI archive shots of lifeboat in action

Monitoring the impact

In seeking to match those various digital effects, the writer must always be reading back the words he has put on the page and monitoring how strongly they achieve the same impact – how easily they translate to a screen in his mind. Has he created walking, talking images of real people and real places or merely put ink on paper? Has he got the right mix of those four basic ingredients?

(for **Visuals**)   (for **Information**)   (for **Sounds**)   (for **Action**)

Which makes for an easily remembered acronym: **VISA**

Properly deployed, these elements constitute a pattern of hallmarks guaranteeing excellence for the journalist in whatever sphere of this digital age.

3 The Writer as Cameraman

Creating words that make pictures depends very much on the writer being able to examine subjects and settings as if from behind a camera

Alison Kervin took a strikingly visual approach in her interview for *The Times* with someone who could claim to be the greatest sportsman on earth.

See below how in doing so she achieved a well-balanced distribution of the four elements of VISA. If the resulting pattern proves pleasing to the eye, the feature has been well constructed.

The Power and the glory

The Kervin Interview

PHIL TAYLOR

Phil Taylor sits back in his armchair and folds his arms. A shaky tattoo is bunched up in the crook of his left arm. It resembles the sort of thing he might have done himself. "The Power", it says, in blue ink and it crawls from his biceps to his lower arm. "The Power" is also printed on his T-shirt, on his new car and on trophies cluttered together at the back of his ornament-filled living-room.

As Taylor points over to the mug of tea on the flowery carpet by his feet, it is not instantly apparent why this man would claim to have more "power" than any other 40-year-old. He has his stockinged feet stretched out ahead, the remote control by his side and the athletics on the television. He takes a large slurp of his tea and sits back to marvel at the brilliance of the events being performed in front of him. What power?

To see Taylor competing is to see a man with a real skill at work. Someone able to psyche out opponents, send them crashing out of every competition in which he participates and able to win everything, all over the world, all the time. He is so far advanced in his sport that he has no genuine opposition. He is, arguably, the best sportsman to have lived; he is certainly the most successful darts player in history and, if continued success is a measure of greatness, then the nine-times world Matchplay Champion has a real claim to be the greatest sportsman on earth.

The problem with this, of course, is that this is darts. And before you can begin to consider brilliance, greatness and competitive spirit, you have to disabuse yourself of the notion that darts is not sport. This, in turn, demands a quick analysis of what comprises sport. Can one definition be offered that covers everything from gymnastics to shooting and running to golf? How can hitting a little ball into a hole be sport but throwing an arrow at a board not? If archery and javelin are sports, then darts must be,

unless the definition of sport rides on the size of the implement being thrown.

Darts is a sport because it's tough. It's one on one, it's competitive and it needs concentration and training. "I practise every day. People think darts is finishing, but it's about keeping thinking about everything as much as other athletes do."

Perhaps one of the reasons that it is hard to think of darts in the same way as other sports, such as golf, is because of the context in which it takes place. Golf is played outside, darts is played mostly by overweight men in smoke-filled bars. You think of golf and you think of Tiger Woods striding imperiously towards a flagstick. You think of darts and it conjures up half a dozen thick-set men down the Nag's Head with egg-stained vests and roll-ups between each of their fingers.

"People who think darts is all about drinking are wrong," Taylor said. "It's changed so much since the beginning of the 90s. It's a professional sport now. You can't compete at the higher levels. against the players that are coming through, if you're for ever in the bar. I think I've been in a pub for a drink maybe three times in the last year."

Taylor's most recent victory was on Saturday night when he stormed to victory in the World Matchplay Championship. He finished the championships by performing to thousands who had packed the Blackpool hotel. He managed to smile at his fans, facing them while they screamed and clapped, before spinning round and throwing the final dart to win the match. Pure drama.

His opponent looked on with the same resignation as the dozens of players who had fallen before. No one in world darts can beat Taylor. He has moved ahead of the field that is made up of experts who followed his lead. On Saturday he talked of him winning another nine world titles before anyone is good enough to match him.

The fans whom he has accumu-

lated during his 15-year career would certainly love to see him stay in the game for ever. Taylor is the darts answer to Tiger Woods but Taylor dominates his tournament more at the end of every event and they claim that having him on the bill makes them ten of thousands in increased revenue.

On Saturday night, his fans became so rowdy that Taylor had to be lifted out of the room by burly bouncers. His sleeves torn and the bouncers carried him to safety; then more than 3,000 people chanted for him until he came back into the room.

The following fan is great. It seems that, with the more supporters Taylor had that the British would start supporting him but it doesn't seem to happen like that," he said.

Taylor is respected as much as ever as a darts player but events in his private life years ago threatened to tarnish his image permanently. He was accused of sexually assaulting two 23-year-old female fans after an exhibition match in

Fife and in May this year he was found guilty and fined £2,000 at Dunfermline Sheriff Court. The period from the accusation to the trial are described by Taylor as "the worst two years of my life".

The events leading to the accusation occurred in his motor home. He offered two women a lift home one evening after a darts and the three of them began drinking vodka and coke. The women claimed in court that Taylor then tried to kiss one of them while she was lying on the back seat and that he had "fondled" both women. Taylor denied the charges and is still shaken by the events and is much more wary because of them. He says that he has come to realise his vulnerability and does not want to put himself or his family through such an experience again. Taylor began playing darts in 1986. He used, unusually, going with his friends to a week to a local pub in the CIU League, but far from the beginning that he had a natural talent for it — "a good arm" — and a year later joined the Super

League. After just a few games, he was selected to represent Staffordshire. Taylor started playing four or five times a week. In 1988, he came to the attention of Eric Bristow, who agreed to sponsor him for two years on the condition that Taylor paid him back when he started earning money.

"I was a sheet-metal worker at the time, making around £250 a week, which was a lot back then," he said. "I was terrified at the thought of giving up work but I did. I packed up my job on Friday, panicked all weekend and started another job on Monday because I was so worried about what would happen to us as a family. I only did that job for a while before I realised that I was being offered a once-in-a-lifetime opportunity in darts and found the guts to give up work for good."

It paid off. Just two years later, in 1990, he became the world champion and in the 11 subsequent years he has won it nine times.

These days he makes a lot of money — Taylor estimates that in an average year, he earns about £200,000 from prize-money and sponsorship. He confesses that a few days ago he got into his new car and went for a drive past the factory where he used to work. He saw the workers coming out for their lunch break, in overalls, covered in dust.

He had been there the morning practising darts and was off to a smart leisure club in the afternoon to weight train and swim with friends. "I was feeling low at the time but I looked at them and realised how far I'd come," he said.

Two any farther, Taylor thinks he needs some good, regular competition. He recognises that there are excellent darts players coming through a system but that at present there is no one to challenge. He need a tough competitor, he said. "Darts is in the mind and you need to be under pressure to throw your best."

Taylor has the mind game of darts down to a fine art. He consciously sets himself apart from the

other players. He does not drink with them on tours and, if they are standing at the bar, he will be away joins them but never joins them.

"Familiarity breeds contempt," he said. "I want to be different. I was talking to Barry Hearn [the promoter] about this and he told me the tale of a young snooker player who wanted to be feared. He organised a limo to drop him off outside the competition venue and he had a porter to take his bags. As the other guys were clambering out of taxis, he was dressed smartly getting his bags carried. People ask, 'who's that?' straight away and they're worrying about you already. I can see when people play me that they're worried. I can see the fear in their eyes and I know I've got them."

Taylor makes a point of studying his best darts opponent as soon as he looks down. He watches him in there, humiliating him. "It's like boxing. You've got to get your guy."

Taylor is as others of his ability to go on for another ten years. He believes that there is much he can still do in darts. He loves the sport more than ever and wants to secure about the future. He wants within the sport and sponsor a young talent, in the same way that Bristow looked after him.

"It's hard to look into the future because you don't know what will happen," he said. "Eric's still playing but he can't let go of the addition which is a shaky condition that can't get go of the dart. It's a nervous thing and, once you lose it, you lose the mental edge. If that happened to me, I'd give up. I couldn't go out there if I didn't think I was going to win.

"As far as Eric is concerned, there is no shame in coming second. No point is playing up unless you are going to win."

ALISON KERVIN

Phil Taylor sits back in his armchair and folds his arms. A shaky tattoo is bunched up in the crook of his left arm. It resembles the sort of thing he might have done himself. 'The Power', it says, in blue ink and it crawls from his biceps to his lower arm. 'The Power' is also printed on his T-shirt, on his new car and on the trophies cluttered together at the back of his ornament-strewn living-room.

As Taylor reaches for the mug of tea on the flowery carpet by his feet, it is not instantly apparent why this man would claim to have any more 'power' than any other 40-year-old. He has his stockinged feet stretched out ahead, the remote control by his side and the athletics on the television. He takes a large slurp of his tea and sits back to marvel at the brilliance of the events being performed in front of him. What power?

But to see Taylor competing is to see a man with a real skill at work. Someone able to psyche out opponents, send them crashing out of every competition in which he participates and able to win everything, all over the world, all the time. He is so far advanced in his sport that he has no genuine opposition. He is, arguably, the best sportsman to have lived; he is certainly the most successful darts player in history and, if continued success is a measure of greatness, then the man who won the Stan James World Matchplay Championship last weekend and is the nine-times world champion* has a real claim to be the greatest sportsman on earth.

The problem with this, of course, is that this is darts. And before you can begin to consider brilliance, greatness and competitive spirit, you have to disabuse yourself of the notion that darts is not

This Hallmark-coded interview immediately demonstrates the ability of words to make pictures by introducing the subject as if through the eye of a TV camera – first a long shot of the figure in an armchair, then zooming in to examine the tattoo on his arm, then pulling back to reveal the image repeated on his T-shirt, then pulling back still further to show the clutter of trophies in the ornament-strewn living-room. The camera lingers for a while as we establish the social status of a man who slurps tea from a mug while as watching TV with his stockinged feet stretched out across a flowery carpet.

So we have visited Phil Taylor in his home. Now we need to learn why he is known to the outside world as 'The Power' and that information is duly supplied in a manner guaranteed to grab the attention of the most flippant reader. Can this homely chap really be a nine-times world champion – perhaps the greatest sportsman on earth?

Until now we have no idea what he does. That is because this article is being printed in **The Times** *and the writer correctly assumes that its readers would claim not to be faintly interested in a sport that normally inhabits the nether regions of the tabloids and late-night spots on remote TV channels.*

Alison Kervin is demonstrating how to engage the interest of the disinterested. After exercising their curiosity and raising their expectations for 400 words, she is confident they will stay with her when she

*Subsequently won world title seven times more

a sport. This, in turn, demands a quick analysis of what comprises sport. Can one definition be offered that covers everything from gymnastics to shooting and running to golf? How can hitting a little ball into a hole be sport but throwing an arrow at a board not? If archery and javelin are sports, then darts must be, unless the definition of a sport rides on the size of the implement being thrown.

reveals we have been dropping in on a darts player.

And to make sure, the next paragraphs show that she fully understands their prejudices while seeking to persuade them that there might be more to this sport than they think. In fact, Taylor went on to win the world title on seven more occasions.

 I

'Darts is a sport because it's tough. It's one on one. It's competitive, it needs concentration and training,' Taylor said. 'I practise every day. Practising my finishing, thinking about my game.'

 S

That's the cue for the man slumped in the armchair to speak and he provides his personal testimony that darts really is a proper sport and that he regards himself as an athlete.

Perhaps one of the reasons why it's hard to think of darts in the same way as other sports, such as golf, is because of the context in which it takes place. Golf is played outside, darts is played by mainly overweight men in smoke-filled bars. You think of golf and you think of Tiger Woods marching imperiously to glory. Think of darts and it conjures up half a dozen thick-set men down the Nags Head with egg-stained vests and roll-ups between each of their fingers.

V

The writer keeps her still-doubting readers on board by conjuring up two contrasting pictures – Tiger Woods imperiously striding verdant fairways in the great outdoors and the yobboes with egg-stained vests leaning against the bar in the smoke-filled Nag's Head.

'People who think darts is all about drinking are wrong,' Taylor said. 'It's changed so much since the beginning of the 90s. It's a professional game now. You can't compete at the highest level against the youngsters that are coming through, if you are for ever in the bar. I think I've been in a pub for a drink maybe three times in the past year.'

 S

Taylor is allowed to challenge that conception, insisting it's now a professional sport attracting younger players and that he's not a pubgoer.

Taylor's most recent victory was on Saturday night when he stormed to victory in the World Matchplay Championship. He finished the championship by performing to the thousands who had packed out the Blackpool hotel. He turned around to

 A

So far we've had VISUALS (seeing him at home), INFORMATION (learning who he is and what he does) and SOUNDS (hearing his claims for the sport). Now we need to watch him in ACTION and this paragraph does just that. Were it to

smile at his fans, facing them while they screamed and clapped, before spinning round and throwing the final dart to win the match. Pure drama.

His opponent looked on with the same resignation as the dozens of players who had fallen before. No one in world darts can beat Taylor. He has moved so far ahead of the field that the Sky TV experts who followed his match on Saturday talked of him winning another nine world titles before anyone is good enough to match him.

The fans whom he has accumulated during his 15-year career would certainly love to see him stay in the game for that long. Taylor is darts' answer to Tom Jones. The tournament organisers put Taylor on at the end of the night and they claim that having him on the bill makes them tens of thousands in increased revenue.

On Saturday night, his fans became so rowdy that Taylor had to be lifted out of the room by burly bouncers. His shirt was ripped and the bouncers had the sleeves torn off their jackets before they carried him to safety; then more than 3,000 people chanted for him until he came back in the room.

'The following I've got is great. It seems that, the more I win, the more support I get. You'd think that the British fans would start supporting the underdog but it doesn't seem to happen like that,' he said.

Taylor is respected as much as ever as a darts player but events in his private life two years ago threatened to tarnish his image permanently. He was accused of sexually assaulting two 23-year-old female fans after an exhibition match in Fife and in May this year he was found guilty and fined £2,000 at Dunfermline Sheriff Court.

be a television interview, at this point the producer would be rolling a clip of their live coverage of the World Matchplay Championship, capturing the tension of an event being staged in front of a packed audience and the sheer drama of Taylor pausing to tantalize his screaming fans before turning to secure victory with his final dart. *The Times* reader suddenly discovers the armchair man is a flamboyant artist.

That's confirmed when more information about his standing in the game over a 15-year career includes the description that 'Taylor is darts' answer to Tom Jones' – the power of analogy to produce pictures in the mind. In seven words we can imagine this ordinary figure dressed in a sequinned shirt slashed to the waist, cavorting in skin-tight leather pants.

Action again as we witness the mass hysteria his performances can incite.

Invited to comment on this sort of reaction, he modestly thanks his fans. Any sense of ego is well hidden.

The possibility that this interview is in any way developing into an exercise in hero-worship is immediately dispelled by this anecdotal evidence that there is a dark side to the ever-triumphant champion. (Many young writers grateful

The period from the accusation to the trial was described by Taylor as 'the worst two years of my life'.

The events leading to the accusation occurred in his motor home. He offered two women a lift home one evening after the darts and the three of them began drinking vodka and chatting. The women claimed in court that Taylor then tried to kiss one of them while she was lying on the back seat and that he had 'fondled' both women. Taylor denied the charges and is considering appealing. Today he is still shaken by the events and is much more wary because of them. He says that he has come to realise his vulnerability and does not want to put himself or his family through such an experience again.

for the chance to interview someone of distinction play to the image that the subject wishes to present. They should not shirk from exploring less welcome areas especially when, as here, there is a public incident which needs explaining. Questioning need not be hostile but the end result should be a detached view of the subject, in no way effusive.)

Taylor began playing darts in 1986. He started casually, going with his father once a week to a local pub and playing in the CIU League, but it was clear from the beginning that he had a natural talent for it – 'a good arm' – and a year later joined the Super League. After a few games, he was selected to represent Staffordshire. Taylor started playing four or five times a week and, in 1988, he came to the attention of Eric Bristow, who offered to sponsor him for two years on the condition that Taylor paid him back when he started earning money.

Information on his family background and how he came into the game. Biographical details are best kept to about two-thirds of the way through a piece. Readers want to know as much as they can about Taylor's exploits and opinions as the supreme reigning champion before they find out how it all came to be.

'I was a sheet-metal worker at the time, making around £250 a week, which was a lot back then,' he said. 'I was terrified at the thought of giving up work but I did. I packed up my job on Friday, panicked all weekend and started another job on Monday because I was so worried about what would happen to us (the family). I only did that job for a while before I realised I was being offered a once-in-a-

This is Taylor talking but it comes into the Action category because he is describing a happening that marked the big turning point in his life. Anecdotes usually gain by being related in the third person because verbatim accounts all too often simplify the event, lack structure and fail to maximize the potential drama. But here is someone who spins a fine tale.

lifetime opportunity in darts and found the guts to give up work for good.'

It paid off. Just two years later, in 1990, he became the world champion and in the 11 subsequent years he has won the title nine times. These days he makes a lot of money – £17,000 when he won at the weekend – and estimates that, in an average year, he earns about £200,000 in prize money and sponsorship.

Information on a key matter in modern-day sports – how much does the former sheet-metal worker now earn (figures impressive at the time of this article but much inflated since)?

He confesses that a few days ago he got into his new car and went for a drive past the factory where he used to work. He saw the workers coming out for their lunch break, in overalls, covered in dust.

He had just spent the morning practising his darts and was off to a smart leisure club for the afternoon to weight-train and swim with friends. 'I was feeling low at the time but I looked at them and realised how far I'd come,' he said

Part two of the previous anecdote and words that make a vivid picture, enabling us to witness the poignant moment when he drove his new car past the dust-covered workers outside his old factory on his way to the gymnasium and swimming pool. An evocative scene in a rags-to-riches movie.

To go any farther, Taylor thinks he needs some good, regular competition. He recognises there are excellent darts players coming through the system but that at present there is no one to challenge him. 'I can improve a lot as a darts player but I need a tough competitor,' he said. 'Darts is in the mind and you need to be under pressure to throw your best.'

Taylor considers the up-and-coming opposition and laments the lack of a serious rival, delivering a quote that reveals the secret of his success.

Taylor has the mind game of a darts player down to a fine art. He consciously sets himself apart from the other players – he does not drink with them after games and, if they are standing in a huddle at the bar, he will acknowledge them but never join them.

Kervin goes on to describe the mind game which starts with him playing the role of a remote outsider.

'Familiarity breeds contempt,' he said. I want to be different. I was talking to Barry Hearn (the promoter) about this and he told me the tale of a young snooker player who wanted to be feared. He organised a limo

Another fluently told anecdote to explain how he learned to develop this approach. The smartly dressed young player turning up in a limo and calling for a porter to carry his bags to disturb his older

to drop him off outside the competition venue and he had a porter lined up to take his bags. As the other guys were clambering out of taxis, he was dressed smartly having his bags carried. People ask, 'Who's that?' straight away and they're worrying about you already. I can see when people play me that they're worried. I can see the fear in their eyes and I know I've got them then.'

Taylor makes a point of throwing his best darts when his opponent is down. 'As soon as he show weakness, I'm in there, humiliating him,' he said. 'It's like boxing. You need to get your guy on the ropes.'

Taylor is not as sure as others of his ability to go on for another ten years. He believes there is much he can still do in darts. He loves the sport more than ever and wants to train harder and play better. He is not sure about the future. He will stay within the sport and possibly sponsor a young talent, in the same way that Bristow looked after him.

'It's hard to look into the future because you don't know what will happen,' he said. 'Eric's still playing but he has dartitis (a shaky condition where players can't let go of the dart). That's a nervous thing and, once you've had it, you lose the mental edge. If that happened to me, I'd give up. I couldn't go out there if I didn't think I was going to be the best.'

As far as Taylor is concerned, there is no point in coming second. No point in turning up unless you are going to win.

A opponents who had merely arrived by taxi.... Another classic movie scene and we now know that Taylor has always seen himself playing the part of the precocious upstart.

S *A test for the imagination in visualizing a man who stands in front of a dartboard and hurls punches into his opponent's ribs.*

I *Taylor ponders his future.*

S *A rare glimpse of frailty as he confesses a fear of losing his mental edge*

Finally, Alison Kervin delivers her assessment of the man she brought close enough for us to study the tattoo on his arm, of the champion we've been able to watch in action and of the ex-factory worker we've witnessed fleeing from a mob of hysterical fans.

When Rachel Cooke was assigned to do a story on the same Phil Taylor (now ten-times champion) for the *Observer Sunday Magazine*, she took a different approach. Whereas Alison Kervin had taken her cameraman's eye into the heart of his home, Rachel elected for more of an outside broadcast production in joining him on a series of personal appearances in the North Country, travelling side by side in the VW van known as The Power Bus, watching him trying to find challengers in half-empty pubs, staying overnight with him in modest B&Bs.

And what better way to open the action than her word picture of receiving a darts lesson from the man himself in a run-down boozer on a tired-looking main road in Heaton, Newcastle upon Tyne?

> 'Come on,' says my teacher, Phil 'The Power' Taylor, 10 times darts champion of the world. 'You know you can do it. Turn your body to the side. Hold your darts against your belly. That's what you've got a belly for … FOLLOW THROUGH!'
>
> Clunk. My first dart hits the wire. Clunk. So does my second. My third, amazingly, sticks – though not in the board but on the wall behind.
>
> 'Don't worry, duck,' says Taylor. 'You're not the worst I've played. There was one much worse than you.'
>
> Casually, he throws his own arrows. They stack up, neatly, like ticks in a school register. 'But his name was Stevie Wonder.'
>
> Taylor pauses, takes in the momentarily blank look on my face, and begins tittering, Muttley-style.
>
> 'Heh, heh, heh,' he wheezes.
>
> When Taylor makes a joke, there is very little you can do but patiently spread a Zen-like grin across your face and count slowly to ten. His gags … are so creaky and rehearsed, you half-expect him to brandish a couple of cue cards with the words 'AUDIENCE: LAUGH NOW' emblazoned on them.
>
> 'Geddit? Stevie Wonder! Hee, hee, hee …'

In what might be termed the 'rolling interview', the writer achieves the intimacy of a fly-on-the-wall TV documentary, the subject is always 'on screen' and gradually becomes unaware of the observer (the writer having the enormous advantage of filming mentally, without the presence of an actual camera and crew).

The result of this up-close-and-personal relationship is that description takes on a familiarity denied the armchair interview:

Interviewing a subject over the course of several days and in varying locations provides a greater chance of personal observation but still needs the basic elements of Visuals, Information, Sounds and Action

Short – he is 5ft 7ins – and pale of skin, Taylor weighs in at between 15 and 20 stone, depending on how determinedly he has managed to stick to his favoured dietary regime of Ryvita and cottage cheese (his great weakness is chicken chow mein). The forearms are muscular but the rest of him sags hopelessly, his stomach spilling over his belt like so much over-ripe brie.

This evening, he is wearing a shiny Port Vale shirt the same colour, and size, of a Girl Guide tent and voluminous black trousers. On his feet are a pair of voluminous white trainers: caught in the dark swirl of the pub's dirty carpet, they gleam like a couple of expensive yachts.

Far removed from a PR-staged setting is Rachel's account of a B&B breakfast during their time on the road:

> In the morning, I'm busy attacking an oily mattress of fried bread, when Taylor appears, one hand placed comfortably on his belly, the other on his groin. No breakfast for him, he says. He does, however, help himself to a soggy kiss, which he lands right on my tightly pursed lips. He has promised to send me my very own set of darts when I get home, a gift he now decides I will receive with an especially naughty kind of excitement.
>
> 'If you and your boyfriend play strip darts like me and Yvonne (his wife), you'll be naked in five minutes,' he says. 'But that's probably what you're hoping, isn't it, Rachel?'

This incident and an episode later in the trip when he accuses the writer of lechery ('the object of my desire: a smelly, half-cut, sixtysomething Scouser') enables Rachel to probe deeply into the matter of his conviction of indecent assault on two of his women fans. Claiming to have been nearly driven to suicide and vowing redemption, he tells her:

> 'Some women are big and rough. They'll grab your bum or your knackers. But I say: "You'd better not or I'm out of the door."'

Although strong on atmosphere, the feature is loaded with hard information about his career, earning power, family life, a passion for carrying out do-it-yourself home improvements and his dartitis and diabetes medical condition. Its big strength is the variety of scene setting and the sense of intimacy.

Visiting Taylor in his home (Power Towers), Rachel Kervin was able to observe the tattoo on one arm; after days as his travelling companion, Rachel Cooke can list a wizard hurling thunderbolts tattooed on the other arm, Jesus on his right leg, an angel on his back, an eagle on his chest and in an undisclosed location his very first tattoo at the age of 17 – a panther ('because the guy couldn't do zebras').

Unfortunately in these times of cost-cutting editorial budgets, writers are rarely afforded the luxury of living with their subject. In more prosperous days, I was fortunate to be commissioned to produce a series where I spent a whole week with variously an Olympic athlete, a racing driver, a jazz band leader and a top footballer.

On the morning of my last day with racing driver Innes Ireland, he took me into the library of his imposing country home and said: 'I've enjoyed having you along this week but it's time you did some work and actually interviewed me.'

He could not understand that I didn't need to sit down and fire questions at him because I had already accumulated all the answers – revealing quotes gleaned from everyday conversations, behavioural traits observed at first hand, fears and ambitions disclosed over late-night drinks.

Not once did I produce a notebook or recorder. That would have broken the chord we had established. But at the first opportunity whenever out of his sight, I would be scribbling down what I had just seen and heard. And this approach only works when you can make maximum use of that most invisible of recorders – your memory.

If the world's best darts player can style himself The Power, the most successful interviewers can lay claim to the Power of Recall.

The secret of 'fly-on-the-wall' interviews is for the subjects never to be aware that they are being formally interviewed

4 Profiles – Hitting the Target

The Profile is the ultimate exercise in the craft of feature writing. It encompasses all of the necessary skills of Researching, Interviewing, Observing, Assessing and Assembling to produce a balanced assessment

My dictionary describes the profile variously as a short biographical sketch... an outline of the characteristics of a certain type of person... the extent to which the subject's manner, attitude or behaviour attracts attention or reveals feelings and intentions... examination of a public image... especially one created and controlled by design.

A journalistic term coined by the *New Yorker* magazine in the 1920s, the Profile represents a challenge to take the reader behind that public image, to unveil the real person. Since subjects will be well known – otherwise who cares? – either nationally (show business, sport, politics, business) or locally (mayor, chief constable, president of the Women's Institute, master of foxhounds) there is little point in re-presenting a familiar picture.

Not an exercise in for character assassination

This does not imply a Profile is always an exercise in character assassination by way of lurid tabloid-style revelations (although the public has a hearty appetite for the like).

Lynn Barber, a prolific Fleet Street interviewer – dubbed the 'Demon Barber' by celebrities who considered themselves victims of her forthright interrogations – always denied she ever set out to do a 'hatchet job' but would consciously seek to animate dull proceedings:

> My idea of a hellishly boring interviewee, she wrote in her book, *A Curious Career* (Bloomsbury), is one who is obviously nice, sane, polite, who chats pleasantly, is happy to answer your questions and has nothing to hide. Where's the fun in that? Give me a monster every time – someone who throws tantrums, hurls insults, storms out and creates mayhem.

It is not always necessary to go quite so far. Unexpected gentler aspects can be revealing – the hardline international footballer who likes to play the romantic lead in his home town's amateur dramatics... the High Court judge who has a model railway circuit in his private chambers... the gentle civil servant appointed MBE for raising money

The Profile Dartboard represents the circle of enquiries needed to produce a fully rounded picture of your subject

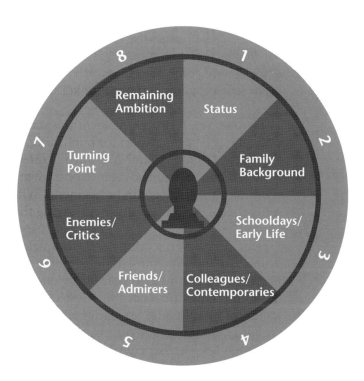

If a profile is to be a well-rounded examination of the subject, the writer needs to score all round this 'Profile Dartboard'. Scoring in each of the eight sections should throw up all the raw material you need. Fashioning it to hit the ultimate target of the bull's eye will depend on three aspects of the writer's input:

Description – bringing the subject to life

Research – bringing their past to life

Assessment – delivering the verdict

for a lifeboat charity who becomes a tyrannical Captain Bligh character when he invites friends on board his surprisingly grand personal yacht…

If the Profile does not surprise in any way it merely colludes with the public image. Or you have chosen a dull subject.

Establishing why your subject is worthy of a mini-biography is the first of eight scoring zones on your Profile Dartboard.

1 You have to establish his/her newsworthy status. Above all there must be a topical peg, a reason for publishing at this time: The latest triumph? A rare failure? A change of direction? A new film, book, play, album, TV series, cabinet post? Significant anniversary? A career milestone? Impending retirement? Without any of these elements the piece will lack urgency, leaving the reader wondering: Why now?

The remaining seven scoring zones complete a circle of enquiries that alone can provide a fully rounded picture of your subject.

The famous queue up to appear on TV chat shows all over the world. But no matter how deep the host's preliminary research or his guile at questioning, no matter whether on camera for 10 minutes or an hour, the outcome can never be no more than just another interview – an experience strictly in one dimension since the viewers will only see and hear whatever the celebrity chooses to reveal about him or herself. And no more. He/she is the single source of information.

In contrast, a long-running and highly popular TV programme of yesteryear called *This Is Your Life* used to sit the celebrity in the heart of the studio and then confront him with a procession of people from every part of his life, each emerging in turn through a central doorway and contributing a personal insight into his character and personality.

That was the nearest to having a Profile enacted before our eyes and it's an image the feature writer should keep in mind when trying to bring someone to life in print.

Like a barrister summoning a string of character witnesses, make sure your copy accommodates a stream of people coming into view who can deliver a variety of anecdotes that provides a 360-degree view of your subject's life.

Aimed at a family audience on a mainstream channel, *This Is Your Life* tended to be cosy rather than astringent, the contributions mainly praiseworthy, rarely objective. (Although a presenter of TV's *Crimewatch* was revealed as having a police record and a famous footballer ran away from the studio for fear of being exposed as

The profile writer must think of himself as a barrister summoning a string of character witnesses to build up an all-round picture of his subject

conducting an extra-marital affair)

So in visualizing the *This Is Your Life* format, make sure you dig deeper and harder in working your way around those seven other zones on the Profile Dartboard:

2 Are there any skeletons in the family closet? Was it a happy home? Well or badly behaved? How did his/her siblings see him/her?

3 What kind of education? Good scholar or a rebel? Bullied or a bully? How do his teachers remember him/her?

4 Any difference in the views of people who knew him/her at the beginning of their career and presently? Extra-mural activities? Memories of former girl/boyfriends?

5 What qualities win friends and admirers? Do they share the public image?

6 What characteristics provoke dislike? How is he/she rated by their critics?

7 Most successful people can identify the most significant point in their career. What was it?

8 Establishing what else the subject wants from life, what ambition remains to be fulfilled, will often provide an unexpected and revealing insight which can challenge the established image.

So that's what you are aiming for – there's your 'dartboard'. And let's assume you have three 'darts'. The way in which you deliver them will determine how successfully you hit the target.

description

Dart A is the ability to produce Visuals which bring the subject to life – not only their physical attributes but any significant mannerisms or behavioural traits and both their public and private persona.

Dart B is the ability to garner a range of anecdotes that show the subject in Action and vividly illustrate each element of the evidence you have assembled. Without anecdotes your Profile is merely a rapidly fading scrapbook of still photographs; with anecdotes it becomes a colourful DVD.

Dart C is the bull's-eye delivery because this is how you come up with

How much does the image provided by friends and admirers compare with that of people who have reasons to dislike your subject?

Unearthing an unexpected remaining ambition can reveal a totally different aspect of a familiar figure

A profile of an established celebrity without any surprising revelations is merely reprinting a familiar portrait

your final Assessment, the overall picture you wish to leave with the reader. A Profile promises to reveal the real person – not necessarily the image in public circulation.

A measure of the degree to which you have succeeded will be a reader finishing the piece with the thought:

'Well, I would never have thought that…!'

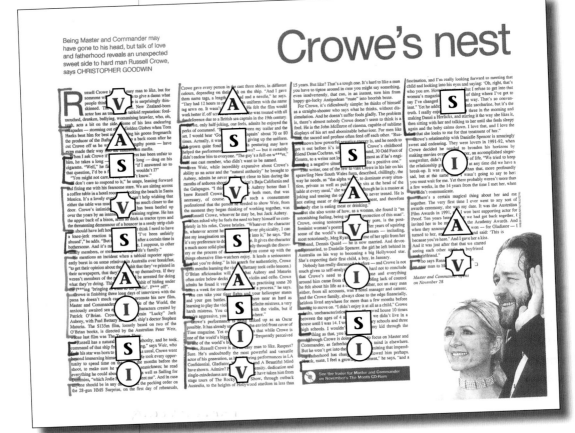

Now let's see how closely this *Sunday Times* profile by Christopher Goodwin of a Hollywood hell-raiser hits the target

Like most journalists featured in this book, Rachel Cooke and Christopher Goodwin make free use of the Historic Present tense – describing something that has happened as if still happening. It is the difference between readers feeling that they are there sharing the moment with the writer or waiting for him to come back and tell them what he discovered – the difference between the sensation of actually walking in on Taylor and finding him in his armchair or hearing about it by way of a visit from a third party. Historic Present is most used in dialogue, action sequences and description of characters and settings; background information and anecdotal passages will revert to Past tense.

Russell Crowe is not an easy man to like, but for someone who doesn't seem to give a damn what people think about him, he is surprisingly thin-skinned. The 39-year-old New Zealand-born actor has an unenviable tabloid reputation: foul-mouthed, drunken, bullying, womanising brawler, who, oh yeah, acts a bit on the side.

Some of his less endearing escapades – storming out of the Golden Globes when Tom Hanks beat him for best actor, having his goons frogmarch the producer of the Bafta awards into a back room after he cut Crowe off as he was reading a lengthy poem – have made their way into mainstream media.

When I ask Crowe if he feels the press has been unfair to him, he takes a long – an ominously long – drag on his cigarette. 'Well,' he finally answers, 'if I answered no to that question, I'd be a f***ing moron, wouldn't I?'

'You might not care,' I say. 'I don't know.'

'I don't care to respond to it,' he snaps,

The writer opens with the obvious – a blunt description of the film star with a reputation for boorish behaviour familiar to millions of tabloid readers. But he balances this with the promise of a surprising revelation – that the New Zealander is not as tough as you might think. The reader is immediately engaged. This is clearly not just another rehash of Crowe's hell-raising legend.

Having stated that the man is prone to misbehave, two brief anecdotes prove it with glimpses of Crowe in action.

Time for the subject to speak. Unless a celebrity writer who wants to emphasize his presence, the interviewer is advised to be unseen and unheard, a purveyor of information and not a performer. In general, readers prefer answers to questions rather than having to wait while the question is spelled out first. It saves precious words and speeds up the flow. Here the conversation is deliberately given in full because it is the way Crowe reacts that is significant – the ominously long drag on his cigarette before he finally refuses to answer and then crudely poses a question of his own.

Without that description, Crowe's answer might have read as an immediate retort. Which the reply to the second question most certainly was – Crowe snapping back at the interviewer. It's an exchange that can be clearly visualized. Together they signal a man who is not an easy conversationalist. A bald statement that Russell Crowe declined to comment on press attitudes towards him could not possibly convey the vehemence of his attitude.

leaning forward and fixing me with his fearsome stare. We are sitting across a coffee table in a hotel room overlooking the beach in Santa Monica. It's a lovely evening, but I can't help wishing the table was much bigger or I was much closer to the door. Crowe's intimidating presence has been beefed up over the years by an intense weight-training regime. He has the upper back of a bison, arms as thick as tractor tyres and the threatening demeanour of a bouncer in a seedy strip club you should have left hours ago.

V — A vivid description of Crowe's intimidating physique – 'the upper back of a bison, arms as thick as tractor tyres and the threatening demeanour of a bouncer in a seedy stripclub you should have left hours ago.' This is colourful analogy at its finest. Suddenly you can both picture the man and feel his presence.

'I don't think I have to have a knee-jerk reaction to it and say: "I've been unfairly abused"' he adds. 'But the weight of it after a certain time is bothersome. And it's more bothersome, I suppose, to other family members, or members of my wife's family.'

S — *Crow resents his surveillance by the media and goes on to demonstrate forcibly just why.*

He mentions an incident when a tabloid reporter apparently burst in on some relatives in Australia over breakfast, 'to get their opinion about the bullshit that they've printed in their newspapers, that they've made up themselves. If they weren't members of the press, they'd be arrested for doing what they're doing. This cowardly bullshit of hiding under the f***ing "bringing of truth to the public'. F*** off".'

A — Strong language in his own description of an incident which explains his hatred of the press.

Crowe is finishing three long days of interviews with the press he doesn't much care for, to promote his new film, *Master and Commander: The Far Side of the World*, the anxiously awaited sea epic based on characters created by Patrick O'Brian. Crowe plays Captain 'Lucky' Jack Aubrey, with Paul Bettany as his foil, ship's doctor Stephen Maturin. The $135 million film, loosely based on two of the O'Brian books, is directed by the Australian Peter Weir, whose last film was *The Truman Show*.

I — *Now comes a solid block of information about the starring role in his latest film and the size of the budget financing its director, Peter Weir – the first contribution from an acquaintance.*

'Russell has a natural energy and authority, and he took command of that ship from the beginning,' says Weir, who feels his star was born to play the role.

A quote from Weir introduces more information, revealing Crowe's obsession with immersing himself in his part.

As usual, Crowe went beyond immersing himself in the part. He took every opportunity to spend time on the sea in the months before the shoot, to make sure he wouldn't get seasickness; he read everything he could about the period, as well as *Sailing for Dummies*, 'which Jodie Foster kindly sent me'.

An illustration of the preparation he puts into playing a major role.

And in case anybody should be in any doubt about the pecking order on the 28-gun HMS *Surprise*, on the first day of rehearsals, Crowe gave every person in the cast three shirts, in different colours, depending on their rank on the ship.

'And I gave them name tags, a length of thread and a needle,' he says. 'They had 12 hours to report back in uniform with the name tags sewn on. It wasn't for my ego.' He felt the film would work better if, off screen as well as on, he was treated with all the deference due to a British sea captain in the 19th century.

Crowe, only half-joking, one feels, admits he enjoyed the perks of command.

A

Crowe provides an example of the lengths to which he went to portray a British sea captain, claiming (not entirely convincingly) that pulling rank on the actors playing his crew 'wasn't for my ego'

'Every day, between my trailer and the set, I would hear 'Good morning, Captain' about 70 or 80 times. Actually, it was quite difficult giving up the uniform. I'd grown quite fond of it.'

All this posturing may have helped the performance – who knows? – but it certainly didn't endear him to everyone.

'The guy's a full-on w***er,' said one cast member, who didn't want to be named.

Confirmation of his contradictory character when he goes on to admit he enjoyed the deference shown to him by the rest of the cast although his 'posturing' produced this resentful quote from one cast member. For a profile to attain balance and objectivity it needs some critical input, preferably from a named source. The wish to remain anonymous reveals the fear engendered by the Crowe regime.

Even Weir, while incredibly expansive about Crowe's ability as an actor and the 'natural authority' he brought to Aubrey, admits he never really got close to him

Weir describes the difficulty in getting to know the real Russell Crowe when he takes on his screen identity.

during the months of arduous shooting in Mexico's Baja California and the Galapagos. 'I think I knew Jack Aubrey better than I knew Russell Crowe,' he says. For both men, that was necessary, of course. Crowe is such a consummate professional that the person he needed to show Weir, from the moment they began thinking of working together, was not Russell Crowe, whoever he may be, but Jack Aubrey.

When asked why he feels the need to bury himself so completely in his roles, Crowe bristles. 'Whatever the character is, whatever accent he requires, whatever physicality, I can use my imagination and jump straight into it,' he says. 'But it's my preference to do the preparation. It gives the character a much more solid platform, and it's only through the discovery or the process of discovery that you come up with the things obsessive film-watchers enjoy. It lends a seriousness to what you're doing.'

S *As a further glimpse of his short temper, Crowe 'bristles' at being asked to spell out his approach to acting but then gives a well-reasoned account of his methods.*

In his search for authenticity, Crowe spent months learning the violin. (Bettany took cello lessons.) O'Brian aficionados will know that Aubrey and Maturin often retire below decks to play the violin and cello. Crowe admits he found it difficult, even practising some 20 hours a week for months.

A Having recorded that he is obsessive, the profile needs to prove it. And the result is a further anecdote which does just that – followed by his explanation of the process involved, revealing the sensitivity he had to acquire in learning to play the violin.

'It's a hell of a process,' he says. 'You can take your tiger fights and your helicopter stunts and your gun battles. They're nowhere near as hard as learning to play the violin. It's a very definite mistress. You can be strong with the violin, but if you're aggressive, you won't get anywhere.'

S *The hell-raising Hollywood hero admits 'if you're aggressive, you won't get anywhere'. Not something to be expected of a man with arms as thick as tractor tyres.*

Crowe's performance is being talked up as an Oscar possible. It has already secured him the envied front cover of Time magazine. Yet even Time notes that while Crowe is one of the world's biggest stars, he is 'frequently perceived as one of the

I *Another critical view of the actor being tipped for an Oscar,* Time *magazine noting that the man successful enough to be put on their cover is 'frequently perceived as one of the world's biggest jerks'.*

world's biggest jerks'.

Yes, Russell Crowe is not an easy man to like. Respect? Sure. He's undoubtedly the most powerful and versatile actor of his generation, as his blistering performances in *LA Confidential*, *Gladiator*, *The Insider* and *A Beautiful Mind* have shown. Admire? Perhaps. His intensity, dedication and single-mindedness are astonishing, and have taken him from stage tours of *The Rocky Horror Show*, through outback Australia, to the heights of Hollywood stardom in less than 15 years. But like? That's a tough one. It's hard to like a man you have to tiptoe around in case you might say something, even inadvertently, that can, in an instant, turn him from happy-go-lucky Antipodean 'mate' into boorish brute.

For Crowe, it's ridiculously simple: he thinks of himself as a straight-shooter who says what he thinks, without dissimulation. And he doesn't suffer fools gladly. The problem is, there's almost nobody Crowe doesn't seem to think is a fool. He is the John McEnroe of the cinema, capable of sublime displays of his art and abominable behaviour. For men like that, the sacred and profane often feed off each other.

'Russell knows how powerful negative energy is, and he needs to get it out before it's important,' said Crowe's childhood friend Dean Cochran, who plays in his band, 30 Odd Foot of Grunts, to a writer not long ago. 'It's almost as if he's engineering a negative situation to prepare for a positive one.'

That writer, one of the few to visit Crowe in his lair on his sprawling New South Wales farm, described, chillingly, the way he needs, as the 'alpha wolf', to dominate every situation, private as well as

V

That comment is promptly balanced by listing the acting accomplishments of a dedicated actor. His tendency to behave like a 'boorish brute' off screen leads the writer to describe him as 'the John McEnroe of cinema' (an imaginative phrase), someone capable of sublime displays of his art and abominable behaviour.

S

Profiles need to chart the past and a childhood friend identifies Crowe's negative energy.

A woman writer tells of 'the alpha wolf' who dominates life at Crowe's Australia farm, treating friends and acquaintances

public. 'He sits at the head of the table at every meal,' she wrote, 'and though he is a master at joking and teasing the other men, he is never teased. He is not eating meat or drinking at the moment, and therefore nobody else is eating meat or drinking.'

But she also wrote of how, as a woman, she found it 'an astonishing feeling, being under the protection of this man'. Crowe, oozing testosterone from every pore, is the post-feminist woman's poster boy, though, after years of squiring some of the world's most famous actresses – including, most notoriously, Meg Ryan at the time of her split from her husband, Dennis Quaid.

He is now married. And devotedly married to Danielle Spencer, the girl he left behind in Australia on his way to becoming a big Hollywood star. She's expecting her first child, a boy, in January.

Nobody has really discussed it before – and Crowe is not much given to self-analysis – but it's hard not to conclude that Crowe's need to control everyone and everything around him came from the deeply troubling lack of control he felt about his life as a child. His father, not any easy man either, by all accounts, was a hotel manager and caterer, and the Crowe family, always close to the edge financially, seldom lived anywhere for more than a few months before having to move on.

'I didn't enjoy it at all as a child,' Crowe admits, uncharacteristically open. 'I moved house 10 times between the ages of 4 and 14. In fact, we didn't live in a house until I was 14.

'I went to six primary schools and three high schools. I wouldn't want to put my kid through the same thing as that, you know.'

Although Crowe is doing his best to focus on *Master and Commander*, as fatherhood

in much the same manner he pulled rank on his fellow actors while making the naval film.

 The woman's description of a man 'oozing testosterone from every pore'.

(I) Information on his present family life and his troubled childhood.

S *Looking ahead to fatherhood Crowe insists that any child of his will have a different upbringing.*

looms, his mind is elsewhere. But he won't get into the business of admitting that impending fatherhood has changed him, mellowing him perhaps.

The professional actor is reluctant to consider the implications of a domestic role.

'Look, mate, I feel a growing excitement,' he says, 'and fascination, and I'm really looking forward to meeting that child and looking into his eyes and saying: "Oh, right, that's who you are. How interesting." But I refuse to get into that women's magazine, tabloid sort of thing where I've got to say I've changed this way or that way. That's so convenient.' Yet he adds: 'It sounds a little saccharine, but it's the truth. I really enjoy getting up at three in the morning and making Danni a Horlicks, and stirring it the way she likes it, then sitting with her and talking to her until she feels sleepy again and the baby calms down.

Proof of tenderness behind the tough-guy image – a confession of excitement at the prospect of fatherhood provides the big surprise of the profile. Although insisting he won't 'get into that women's magazine, tabloid thing' he admits that looking forward to looking into a new-born baby's eyes might sound 'a little saccharine'.

'I love that, and I love the fact that she looks to me for that treatment of her.'

Crowe's relationship with Danielle Spencer is amazingly sweet and endearing. They were lovers in 1991 – 92, when Crowe decided he needed to broaden his horizons by making movies overseas. Spencer, an accomplished singer-songwriter, didn't want that kind of life.

'We tried to keep the relationship going, but never at any time did we have a break-up. It was much sadder than that, more profoundly sad, but at the same time I wasn't going to say to her you must wait for me. Yet there weren't probably more than a few weeks, in the 14 years from the time I met her, when we didn't communicate.

Background to his relationship with Danielle Spencer.

'There's a certain magical thing about her and me together. The very first time I ever went to any sort of awards ceremony, she was my date. It was the Australian Film Awards in 1991, and I won best supporting actor for *Proof*. Ten years later, before we

Crucial anecdote of when their romance renewed – with a sentimental quote of explanation from him.

had got back together again, I invited her to be my date for the Academy Awards. And when they announced that I had won – for *Gladiator* – I turned to her, and I leant down and said: "This is because you're here." And I gave her a kiss. And it was just after that that we started seeing each other again as boyfriend and girlfriend.'

Who says Russell Crowe is not an easy man to like?

The writer's assessment. Having assembled the evidence for and against Russell Crowe, the writer has established that there is a soft side to the screen's tough guy.

The subject rightly occupies the bull's-eye of our Profile Dartboard but there are occasions when a profile has to be completed although the personality is not (or chooses not to be) available.

When Gay Talese was commissioned by *Esquire* magazine to write an article on Frank Sinatra he was assured a meeting in Hollywood had been arranged with the notoriously difficult star. But when he arrived he was told the meeting was off because 'Frank Sinatra has a cold'.

That became the title of one of the most famous features in American journalism because, undeterred, Talese spent the next month following Sinatra wherever he went – into a recording studio, on to a film set, into a gambling saloon, into a night club. Lurking in the shadows, he witnessed Sinatra rowing with a TV director, then turning on the charm with showgirls while at the same time instilling fear in those around him. He spoke to nearly 100 people in all, from Sinatra's body-double and his favourite bartender to Sinatra's mother and Frank Junior.

He never did get to interview the subject of his story. Yet his fanatical research made the readers of the 15,000-word finished piece feel they travelled all the way with him – and in doing so they had met the real Frank Sinatra.

Now, let's take a look at how the *Guardian*'s Maeve Kennedy – lacking the luxury of a month-long work cycle – produced a rather more hurried profile of an absent Helen Mirren and still managed to score all round the Profile Dartboard.

The briefest of profiles can be all-encompassing. A few brisk paragraphs are able to accommodate a lengthy career – and capture the lively personality behind those many roles

66 What she has is truth, truth to the text, truth to the role ... she's not afraid to look vulnerable or to let lines show 99

Yet more award ceremonies beckon for inspirational queen of stage and screen

Maev Kennedy

At the Venice film festival the winner of the best actress award was introduced as Her Majesty, Helen Mirren, and as a truly regal progress accelerates towards the Oscars, that looks about right.

At 60 she has never been more in demand – "incredible, isn't it?" she said in a recent interview – but even she seemed to be wearying slightly of the merry-go-round of awards ceremonies: she was pictured this week in stockinged feet, brandishing her shoes in the air at yet another triumph.

Her feet may have hurt, but it won't have been weariness. Stephen Frears, the equally profligately nominated director of The Queen, just off one plane and about to board another, said yesterday: "She just has the most incredible energy, I've never known anyone like her. She leaves the rest of us just standing.

"She is very, very good at what she does, and is serious about her work – but she can have fun too. She's always out raving, or drinking, or travelling, or having a good time. She's a tough cookie, she's had a tough life. She's a sharp, sensible, serious person – but she's absolutely not one for sitting at home with the knitting needles, the complete opposite of me."

Gongs will drop if she, he, and The Queen don't figure heavily among the nominations for the British Academy Awards and the Golden Globes on Monday, always a reliable predictors for next month's Oscars, where Variety has her her "a shoo in" for best actress.

Her life has been measured out in

queens: Elizabeths I and II, mad King George's anguished Charlotte, Morgana la Fey, Lady Macbeth ("Miss Mirren plays everyone else off the stage" one critic wrote, and the stars that she and her Macbeth, Ian McKellen, were not bestest friends punctuating her career at 18, in the 30s for the RSC and in her 50s for the National Theatre, Cleopatra.

It began, as it has for so many British stars, with the National Youth Theatre, where artistic director Paul Roseby described her as "an absolute inspiration" to the company's young women actors. "What she has is truth, truth to the text, truth to the role, she doesn't let femininity get in the way, she's not afraid to look vulnerable to stuttering, or to let lines show. She is very sexy, but it's not a cosmetic Hollywood sexy – it's a fresh-air natural sexiness like somebody you might just see in the street."

She quickly gained a reputation for shining performances in plays and films which were sometimes stinkers, and for shedding her clothes on stage and screen with pleasure, as in Ken Russell's Savage Messiah, the infamous Gore Vidal-scripted, Penthouse magazine-backed Caligula.

But by her early 40s she felt her career had run into the sand – and then she met Jane Tennison of la Plante's tough-talking, chain-smoking television cop, giving and taking no quarter in a man's world.

Prime Suspect reinvented her career: the first was in 1990, the final, bitter, enforced retirement only last year. One of her most famous lines, taken by La Plante straight from a real woman detective, was: "Don't call me ma'am, I'm not the bloody Queen."

Yesterday La Plante said: "Helen has a very rare quality – she has a physical weight. By that I don't mean she's

overweight: it is an asset that few actresses possess. I think it is also the reason why she can play such very strong women, because she is a very sensual and sexual woman she can also portray the feminine side. I always wanted her for the character Jane Tennison because of the above qualities."

Last year the real Queen beckoned. On paper it was an improbable star vehicle, a drama based on the hysterical public mourning and private politicking after the death of Princess Diana, when the Queen, who once greeted her small son after an absence with a firm handshake, stayed behind closed gates at Balmoral. It may seem insane now that people suggested the survival of the monarchy was at stake, but it didn't in those hectic weeks.

The film could have been either risible or creepily obsequious. It was neither: one visitor to the set was left blushing furiously at the strength of her urge to curtsy as she swept into the room in character. It became the year's biggest and most unexpected popular and critical hit.

Mirren spent hours studying film of the Queen's public appearances to get that straight-backed, taut, rigidly controlled manner absolutely correct. She maintained the character even when preparing for a dressing gown and hairnet part. The iron grey waves, which had moments when it all slipped, when she ran up the stairs of the palace, desperate for advice, calling "Mummy?", both startling and touching.

On the one occasion when they actually met, taking together after Dame Helen collected her honour at the palace, she found together more relaxed woman who described the Queen as "charming, twinkly and funny". The Queen has yet to comment.

The CV

Born Ilynea Lydia Mironoff on July 26 1945, second of three children. Her father settled in Essex after being exiled from Russia.
Married Taylor Hackford, 1997.
Education St Bernard's Convent School for Girls, Westcliff-on-Sea, Essex
Career Joined Royal Shakespeare Company in 1967, then starred in films including Caligula in 1979; The Long Good Friday, 1980; Cal, 1984; The Mosquito Coast, 1986; The Cook, The Thief, His Wife and Her Lover, 1989; The Madness of King George, 1994 (Oscar nominated); Gosford Park, 2001; Calendar Girls, 2003; The Queen, 2006. Starred on TV as DCI Jane Tennison in Prime Suspect 1990-96, 2003 and 2006. Made DBE in 2003.

At the Venice Film Festival the winner of the best actress award was introduced as Her Majesty, Helen Mirren, and as a truly regal progress accelerates towards the Oscars, that looks about right.

At 60 she has never been more in demand – 'incredible, isn't it?' she said in a recent interview – but even she seems to be wearying slightly of the merry-go-round of awards ceremonies: she was pictured this week in stockinged feet, brandishing her shoes in the air at yet another triumph.

Instant picture comes to mind of Helen Mirren, having been introduced as 'Her Majesty', making a regal advance on the awards rostrum at Venice while accelerating her way to an Oscar.

A 60-year-old in stockinged feet brandishing her shoes in the air.

Her feet may have hurt, but it won't have been weariness. Stephen Frears, the equally profligately nominated director of *The Queen*, just off one plane and about to board another, said yesterday: 'She has just the most incredible energy, I've never known anyone like her. She leaves the rest of us guys standing.

'She is very, very, very good at what she does, and very serious about her work – but she likes to have fun too. She's always out raving, or drinking, or travelling, or having a good time. She's a tough cookie, she's had a tough life. She's a sharp, sensible, serious person – but she's absolutely not one for sitting at home with the knitting needles, the complete opposite of me.'

S

A lengthy quote from a colleague begins to put her life into perspective – incredible energy, fun-loving , always out raving or drinking or travelling or having a good time. But a profile needs an objective balance so this is no theatrical gush. Frears reveals she is also sharp, sensible, serious, a tough cookie who's had a tough life. A hard-living, fun-loving actress brought vividly to life.

Jaws will drop if she, he, and *The Queen* don't figure heavily among the nominations today for the British Academy Awards and the Golden Globes on Monday, always seen as reliable predictors for next month's Oscars, where Variety has her as 'shoo in' for best actress.

Her life has been measured out in Queens: Elizabeths I and II, mad King George's anguished Charlotte, Morgana la Fey, Lady Macbeth ('Miss Mirren plays everyone else off the stage,' one critic wrote, amid rumours that she and her Macbeth, Nicol Williamson, were not bestest friends) and, punctuating her career at 18, in her 30s for the RSC and in her 50s for the National Theatre, Cleopatra.

I

The imminent nominations for two big awards provide the reason for the publication of the profile at this time. Profiles need a topical peg to be relevant. This paragraph also lists the range of her regal performances, including the suggestion she could be a difficult Lady Macbeth.

It began, as it has for many British stars, with the National Youth Theatre, where artistic director Paul Roseby described her as 'an absolute inspiration' to the young women actors. 'What she has is truth, truth to the text, truth to the role. She doesn't let femininity get in the way, she's not afraid to look vulnerable, or unflattering, or to let

S

The director who spotted her potential as a young actor describes the talent that led to a great career. Quote from one of her early directors, analysing her acting abilities and her sexiness – while not afraid to look vulnerable, or unflattering, or to let lines show.

lines show. She is very sexy, but it's not a cosmetic Hollywood sexy – it's a fresh-air natural sexiness like somebody you might just see in the street.'

She quickly gained a reputation for shining performances in plays and films which were sometimes stinkers, and for shedding her clothes on stage and on screen with pleasing ease, as in Ken Russell's *Savage Messiah* or the infamous Gore Vidal-scripted, Penthouse magazine-backed *Caligula*.

Having just stated that she is sexy the profile meets the need to prove it by relating two examples of the star shedding her clothes on screen with pleasing ease.

But by her early 40s she felt her career had run into the sand – and then she met Jane Tennison, Linda La Plante's tough-talking, hard-drinking television cop, giving and expecting no quarter in a man's world.

The meeting that was to transform her career.

Prime Suspect reinvented her career: the first was in 1991, the final, bitter, enforced retirement only last year. One of her most famous lines, taken by La Plante straight from a real woman detective, was: 'Don't call me ma'am, I'm not the bloody Queen.'

Helen Mirren delivers a line that was strangely prophetic.

Yesterday La Plante said: 'Helen has a very rare quality – she has a physical weight. By that I don't mean she's overweight: it is an asset that few actors possess. I think it is also the reason she can portray such very strong women, and because she is a very sensual and sexual woman she can also portray the feminine side. I always wanted her for the character Jane Tennison because of the above qualities.'

Further input from Lynda La Plante adds to the overall picture.

Last year the real Queen beckoned. On paper it was an improbable star vehicle, a drama based on the hysterical public mourning and private politicking after the death of Princess Diana, when the Queen, who had once greeted her small son after a long absence with a firm handshake, remained behind closed gates at Balmoral.

Background to the film that was to win her the Oscar.

It may seem insane now that people suggested the survival of the monarchy was at stake, but it didn't in those hectic weeks.

The film could have been either risible or creepily obsequious. It was neither: one visitor to the set was left blushing furiously by the strength of her urge to curtsy as Mirren swept into the room in character. It became the year's biggest and most unexpected popular and critical hit.

How Mirren's performance as the Queen was so powerful that the sight of her sweeping into view made a visitor to the set feel the urge to curtsy.

Mirren spent hours studying film of the Queen's public appearances to get that straight-backed, taut, rigidly controlled manner absolutely correct. She maintained the demeanour, even preparing for bed in pink dressing gown and hairnet protecting the iron grey waves, which made the moments when it all slipped, when she ran up the stairs of the palace, desperate for advice, calling 'Mummy', both startling and touching.

Illustrating the lengths to which she goes to get inside the character she is playing.

On the once occasion when they actually met, taking tea together after Dame Helen collected her honour at the palace, she found an altogether more relaxed woman: the dame described the Queen as 'charming, twinkly and funny'. The Queen has yet to comment.

Having opened the piece with Helen Mirren being hailed as a make-believe queen in Venice, we end with the screen star having tea in Buckingham Palace with the Queen herself. The circle of a short but well-judged profile is neatly complete.

NOTE The layout incorporates a panel briefly listing her personal details, education and acting career. This is a useful device, especially when space is short. With a comprehensive CV available to the reader, the body of the profile can concentrate on mentioning only the more significant events.

Sports profiles are of enormous public interest because they reveal the real man or woman behind what is essentially a one-dimensional image of them in action – whether watched from the sidelines in a stadium or in larger-than-life close-up on a domestic TV screen.

With the subject out of the country, this profile manages only one quote from the star himself yet Paul Weaver of the *Guardian* secures input from five key characters in the life of Jonathan Trott.

Trott ready for serious test against the land where his promise shone

The batsman faces his home country 20 years after revealing his rich talent there, writes **Paul Weaver**

Talent's first blo... the precocious suggestion of a gi... more memorable than its fulfilm... ...ns with Jonathan Trott, who make... overseas Test debut for England in his homeland today.

Trott was eight when his delighted family - South Africans of British descent - realised they might... exceptional talent among them. ...ent is recalled by Kenny Jackson, ...alf-brother, whose first-class record...exceptional but who was something of a legend in the local leagues of the Western Province.

"I am 17 years older than Jonathan, so we didn't play cricket together," he said. "But I would bowl to him and obviously he had a bit of ball sense from the start. He was eight whe... it happened, the day something reall...suck us. I was bowling him long-ho...half-volleys so he could hit the ... I decided to get him out, wh...would mark the end of the session. So I bowled length to him. But this time, instead of patting the ball back to me, he hit it on the up, and it sailed over my head, time and time again. It was a bit of a shock."

The schoolboy Trott would scamper to watch Jackson, Peter Kirsten and Adrian Kuiper batting for Western Province at Newlands in the 80s. "I used to sit on the benches, which were called the oaks - they're grass b...," Trott recalled. "There wasn't ...TV in those days so everyone w... a game. I remember Western Province playing Gauteng, which was Transvaal in those days. It was a three-day game over the New Year and it was packed out. Provincial cricket was ...we had because of apartheid."

Trott, 28, is Kevin Pietersen-lite. He is less outrageously talented, less outspoken and when he walks to the crease under the flag of England, he is not booed like his countryman. But Trott has scored heavily on this ...while Pietersen has floundered. A... ne Test, his name is already on ...m-sheet. Ian Bell, who scored a v... England's Ashes-winning Test at The Oval, is the likeliest to be overlooked should they decide to play only five specialist batsmen. Such is the impact Trott has made in his embryonic international career.

He can play for England because his father, Ian, is English. He initially emigrated to Sou... ...ca to run a sports shop and mar... ...al, Donna. When the family ret... the UK in 2001, so Ian could take u... ...as a cricket coach in Surrey, Jonathan followed them.

...an was one of those eager, average cricketers wh... ...e mainstay of the club game. P... ...an', his friend and contemporar... ...Ian bowled very nice off-spin ...n didn't turn. But he always pitched up at cricket nets with

Jonathan Trott plays through the offside en route to his second-innings 119 against Australia at The Oval
Glyn Thomas/Rex Features

proper white... his real respect for the game, wh... ...ssed on to his son. And Donna w... ...hlete so there are good genes the...

...ike young Trott attended Rondebosch School, 500 yards from Newlands. Cricket always held his interest more than anything else. Hi... ...Andrew Puttick, a left-handed ...atsman who is now on the fringe... South Africa team, says Trott bro... ...e record for the highest number of consecutive Friday evening detentions for not doing his homework. "All he wanted to do was play cricket," he said. "Schoolwork was not his forte."

Trott also had trouble controlling his temper. "He was always in trouble," said Puttick. "He was hot-headed, a cheeky little bugger." Jack... ...n says he covered up many stories a... ...he young Jonathan. "He had a te... ...m. But only when it came to sp...

At school they watched him bat and forgave him his tantrums. "He was so much more talented than everybody else,"

How South African are England's players?

Andrew Strauss
Born Johannesburg
Accent Plummy English
Education Radley College, Oxfordshire
Family Father South African, mother English
Qualification Emigrated aged six
Mindset St John's Wood through and through

Kevin Pietersen
Born Pietermaritzburg
Accent Unusual mash-up of Natal brogue and random Anglo-inflections
Education Maritzburg College
Family Mother from Canterbury, father an Afrikaner
Qualification Under residency rule in 2004
Mindset Would rather be slipping into Boujis and shopping in Regent Street

Jonathan Trott
Born Cape Town
Accent Cape Town
Education Stellenbosch University
Family Father English, mother South African
Qualification From birth through his father. Moved to England in 2002
Mindset Says his heart is now in Birmingham

Matt Prior right
Born Johannesburg
Accent Chummy English
Education Brighton College, Sussex
Family Parents from South Africa
Qualification Emigrated aged 11
Mindset Yearning for Hove
Barney Ronay

Puttick said. "I remember opening the batting and there was an early wicket. He came in No3. He ...only about 11 but he absolutely murd... ...e bowling. After 25 overs I had ab... ...d he had 110. He made it look easy. ...e always had this talent and it's good to see him fulfilling that potential. He took a massive decision [to play for England] and all the best to him. He made the most of his career."

Trott and Puttick played for Rondebosch. Then they played age-group cricket together and repr...ted South Africa in the Under-19 W... ...p in 1999, along with Graeme S... ...acques Rudolph. Trott was coach... ...irsten, his idol, at Western Province. Kirsten says he was reminded of Allan Lamb when he watched the young Trott clump the ball through the leg side with his strong bottom hand.

Eric Symonds, who coached Trott some years later, also saw the on-side trait. "He was 19-20 when I ...aw him but he was not such a dom... ...e player as he's become," he sa... ...ds width to play on the off side. A... ...ng on off-stump or just outside he will play to leg."

Trott still had a temper when he pitched up at Warwickshire in 2002. His former county colleague Trevor Penney, who went on to become England's fielding coach and is no... ...e assistant coach at Western Austra... ...lls the young batsman hurling ...wn on his return to the Warwickshire dressing room and smashing a picture which had been ear-marked for a benefit auction.

"I was one of the senior players, so I'd often have to ...under my wing and calm him ...when he lost the plot," Penney... ...that is something he appears to have sorted out." From hot Trott, so to speak.

Trott's mental strength is evident in his determination to make strong first impressions. H... ...245 on his debut for Warwicks... ...nds, 134 on his Championship ...e following year, and famously scored a Test debut century against Australia as England won the Ashes at The Oval last summer.

When he walks out to bat in this ma... his pare... ...ill be there and his half... ...will be watching ...ough he will be in ...Town for the third Test. Jackson soun... wistfully envious. "W... share the same mother and I wish we...d the same father, but w...he said. "But his fa...I are very good frien...was the guy ...h played with him for hour...and...s. Ian and Donna ...lled more miles mo...tronauts would ...on several trips to Ma...

"Jonathan is mentally... stronger than I ever was as a player. I played purely on talent and ability. I got the mental side of the game wrong but Jon...got that spot on.

"...ed to be like me. He as...e me. He idolised me. But there are certain things I got horribly wrong as a professional cricketer. And he's got them dead right."

Talent's first bloom, the precocious suggestion of a gift, can be more memorable than its fulfilment. So it was with Jonathan Trott, who makes his overseas Test debut for England in his homeland today.

An intro which demonstrates the value of apparent contradiction in engaging the immediate interest of the reader. How can an England player make his overseas Test debut in his homeland? Read on!

Trott was eight when his delighted family – South Africans of British descent – realised they might have an exceptional talent amongst them. The moment is recalled by Kenny Jackson, Trott's half-brother, whose first-class record is unexceptionable but who was something of a legend in the local leagues of the Western Province.

Information on his career and his family background

'I am 17 years older than Jonathan, so we didn't play cricket together,' he said. 'But I would bowl to him and obviously he had a bit of ball sense from the start. He was eight when it happened, the day something really struck us. I was bowling him long-hops and half-volleys so he could hit the ball. Then I decided to get him out, which would mark the end of the session. But this time, instead of patting the ball back to me, he hit on the up, and it sailed over my head, time and time again. It was a bit of a shock.'

We witness the first blooming of that talent as a precocious eight-year-old dispatches the bowling of his 25-year-old half-brother, already making a career as a professional cricketer.

The schoolboy Trott would scamper to watch Jackson, Peter Kirsten and Adrian Kuiper batting for Western Province at Newlands in the 80s. 'I used to sit on the benches, which were called the oaks – they're grass banks now,' Trott recalled. 'There wasn't cricket on TV in those days so everyone would go to a game. I remember Western Province playing Gauteng, which was Transvaal in those days. It was a three-day game over the New Year and it was packed out. Provincial cricket was all we had because of apartheid.'

Here we have the voice of Trott, providing a self-portrait of the schoolboy watching his provincial heroes in the days when apartheid denied South Africa the spectacle of Test cricket.

Trott, 28, is Kevin Pietersen-lite. He is less outrageously talented, less outspoken and when he walks to the crease under the flag of England, he is not booed by his countrymen. But Trott has scored heavily on this tour while Pietersen has floundered. After only one Test, his name is already on today's team-sheet. Ian Bell, who scored a vital 72 in England's Ashes-winning Test at The Oval, is the likeliest to be overlooked should they decide to play only five specialist batsmen. Such is the impact Trott has made in his embryonic international career.

(V) *The phrase 'Kevin Pietersen-lite' immediately suggests a deliberately stolid personality who nonetheless proceeded to out-score his more glamorous teammate.*

He can play for England because his father, Ian, is English. He initially emigrated to South Africa to run a sports shop and married a local, Donna. When the family returned to the UK in 2001, so Ian could take up a job as a cricket coach in Surrey, Jonathan followed them.

(I) *Details of his emerging Test career explain the reason for the apparent contradiction in the intro – his father is English.*

Ian was one of those eager, average cricketers who are the mainstay of the club game. Peter Kirsten, his friend and contemporary, said: 'Ian bowled very nice off-spinners which didn't turn. But he always pitched up at cricket nets with proper whites. He had this real respect for the game, which he has passed on to his son. And Donna was an athlete so there are good genes there.'

The young Trott attended Rondebosch School, 500 yards from Newlands. Cricket always held his interest more than anything else.

[S] *A family friend explains Trott's sporting pedigree.*

His friend Andrew Puttick, a left-handed opening batsman who is now on the fringes of the South Africa team, says Trott broke the record for the highest number of consecutive Friday evening detentions for not doing his homework. 'All he wanted to do was play cricket,' he said. 'Schoolwork was not his forte.'

(I) *We discover he was not an academic schoolboy*

Trott also had trouble controlling his temper. 'He was always in trouble,' said Puttick.

△A Anecdotes confirming such a statement

'He was hot-headed, a cheeky little bugger.' Jackson says he covered up many stories about the young Jonathan. 'He had a temper on him. But only when it came to sport.'

At school they watched him bat and forgave him his tantrums. 'He was so much more talented than everybody else,' Puttick said. 'I remember opening the batting and there was an early wicket. He came in No 3. He was only about 11 but he absolutely murdered the bowling. After 25 overs I had about 40 and he had 110. He made it look easy. He always had this talent and it's good to see him fulfilling that potential. He took a massive decision (to play for England) and all the best to him. He made the most of his career.'

Trott and Puttick played for Rondebosch. Then they played age-group cricket together and represented South Africa in the Under-19 World Cup in 1999, along with Graeme Smith and Jacques Rudolph. Trott was coached by Kirsten, his idol, at Western Province. Kirsten said he was reminded of Allan Lamb when he watched the young Trott clump the ball through the leg side with his strong bottom hand.

Eric Symonds, who coached Trott some years later, also saw the on-side trait. 'He was 19–20 when I first saw him but he was not such a dominant leg-side player as he's become,' he said. 'He needs width to play on the off-side. Anything on off-stump or just outside he will play to leg.'

Trott still had a temper when he pitched up at Warwickshire in 2002. His former county colleague Trevor Penney, who went on to become England's fielding coach and is now the assistant coach at Western Australia, recalls the young batsman hurling his bat down on his return to the Warwickshire dressing room and smashing

make clear that (like every successful profile) this is no hagiography. We discover that the youngster was often in trouble at school and hot-headed at the wicket. Yet his emerging talent was obvious.

Trott's career progresses in his teenage years.

Former coach analyses his batting technique.

Another vivid anecdote revealing Trott's explosive temper – something far from apparent in his current image of the solid, dependable hero in moments of crisis.

a picture which had been earmarked for a benefit auction.

'I was one of the senior players, so I'd often have to take him under my wing and calm him down when he lost the plot,' Penney said. 'That is something he appears to have sorted out.' From hot to Trott, so to speak.

S *A former county colleague provides an explanation for the transformation.*

Trott's mental strength is evident in his determination to make strong impressions. He scored 245 on his debut for Warwickshire Seconds, 134 on his Championship debut the following year, and famously scored a Test debut century against Australia as England won the Ashes at the Oval last summer.

I *Evidence of the mental strength that produces big scores.*

When he walks out to bat in this match his parents will be there and his half-brother will be watching on TV, though he will be in Cape Town for the third Test.

V *Here we glimpse the strength of family support which fostered his career.*

Jackson sounds wistfully envious. 'We share the same mother and I wished we shared the same father, but we don't,' he said. 'But his father and I are very good friends. Ian was the guy who played with him for hours and hours. Ian and Donna have travelled more miles to watch Jonathan play than most astronauts would do on several trips to Mars.

I *His half-brother goes into some detail of the family background.*

'Jonathan is mentally far stronger than I ever was as a player. I played purely on talent and ability. I got the mental side of the game wrong but Jonathan has got that spot on.

'He wanted to be like me, he aspired to be me. But there are certain things I got horribly wrong as a professional cricketer. And he's got them dead right.'

S *A rather wistful quote from the half-brother who admires Trott's success while regretting his own career lacked the same mental strength.*

From childhood episodes to present-day stardom, from revelations by family and acquaintances, from a trouble-maker to a Test batsman of remarkable composure – Paul Weaver has come at his subject from many angles. He could incorporate only one quote from the absentee Jonathan Trott for this profile but had he been given instead hours and hours of a one-to-one interview with his subject he could not have produced a much more comprehensive assessment.

Because it is interviews with others that make for a credible profile.

5 Opening with a Bang

The mantra beloved of estate agents – LOCATION, LOCATION, LOCATION – may equally be applied to the art of conducting The Interview

Basically, an interview is the act of eliciting information from someone else.

For **the reporter** on a rush news story, interviewing may be a fragmentary process – obtaining quotes from eye-witnesses, establishing the sequence of events from the police, calling the hospital to check on the condition of casualties. The recurring question is 'What's happened?'

For **the feature writer,** The Interview takes on capital letters; it becomes a set-piece requiring diligent preparation and due time for execution. And the salient question is 'What kind of person are you?'

All too often, certainly in the case of celebrities, the specified setting is abstract – a chic coffee bar, an impersonal hotel room, even the end of a telephone line.

Invoking the analogy that Words That Make Pictures need to be assembled to provide the visual impact of a TV shooting script, such abstract settings deny the writer this vital dimension. There's nowhere for a camera to zoom and roam.

Being able to establish a significant setting for an interview adds enormously to a sense of atmosphere

Conjuring up both sound and vision

But a tabletop interview in a teashop takes on dramatic significance if the subject is JK Rowling and this is the very teashop where an impecunious single mother created Harry Potter. Plenty of words are made available to conjure up both sound and vision – focusing in turn on the shabby décor and the assortment of regular customers against the clatter of cups and saucers amidst a background babble of conversation. All this persuades the readers that they are there looking in on the birthplace of a literary phenomenon.

On the other hand, interviewing a movie star in the penthouse suite of a five-star hotel cannot possibly create the same sense of immediacy.

Lynn Barber's memoirs reveal she is all too familiar with such frustration:

> All journalists dread the hotel circus, when a film company puts a herd of actors in a hotel for a day to plug their new film and expects them to give interviews from dawn to dusk. They're so zonked by doing

A veteran interviewer describes the horrors of PR-staged encounters and declares her preferred location for more intimate observations

non-stop interviews that they will often repeat an anecdote they've already told you word for word, or start an anecdote then forget the ending. Often they have no idea what country they're in. At least twice (once with Audrey Hepburn, once with Lynn Redgrave) I've felt that my interviewee was so exhausted and emotionally fragile I really should be calling an ambulance rather than asking questions. But still the PR sits there stoney-faced, forcing these poor knackered ponies to jump through their publicity hoops.

Lynn goes on:

Ideally, you should always interview people at home because you can learn so much about them. Are they super-neat or chaotic? Do they have more photographs of their family or themselves? A trip to the loo is often instructive – it's where people put their awards and cartoons of themselves, things they're proud of and want visitors to see without too obviously showing off. If you can go to their own bathroom, rather than the guest cloakroom, better still – look for the pills!

Catching a star at work

Hollywood PRs are particularly unrelenting in dictating time and place but the writer should always strive to secure a more relevant location. How much more revealing it is when an interview catches the Hollywood star at work – as Elaine Lipworth achieved in the *Mail on Sunday's Live Magazine*:

Cockatoo Island is just a 20-minute ride from Sydney Harbour but it feels like the middle of nowhere. Convicts were sent here in the 19th century to build dry docks. You can imagine what they went through. It's 1 a.m. and bitingly cold and a sense of desolation permeates the stone buildings. Beautiful but bleak, this is one of the key locations for *X-Men Origins: Wolverine*, starring Hugh Jackman.

When I arrive for my exclusive set interview, they are in the middle of filming a pivotal scene; Jackman, ripped and rugged as Wolverine, is tearing through a cavernous warehouse. Roaring with animalistic rage, he is laying into his brother, Sabretooth, played by an equally vicious-looking Liev Schreiber. Both are bloodied and sweating; the fighting is visceral. You can almost feel the force of the punches.

There is a macho competition between the two actors, Jackman

Escaping the restrictions placed by PRs on access to their clients is difficult but always worth the effort

explains later, when he stops for a break between takes. 'There is a fair bit of testosterone flying about. We look to see if the other one's fading and then both of us always say, "No, I'm fine, let's go again. Come on, you can hit me harder than that."' He thumps the table with his fist. 'Our first big confrontation is in a bar. I'm at one end, he's at the other and we fly at each other. Then he's on all fours like a cat and he tackles me. I remember thinking that I'd broken a couple of ribs. But I'm an Aussie – getting injured is a point of pride.'

In front of the camera, there's a savage intensity to Jackman's performance. Off screen, he switches out of character and is friendly with everybody in the crew. But at the same time it's apparent he's in complete control of the set – he has a commanding presence and orchestrates every detail of the production

Being first able to watch a top actor in action makes for a more intimate interview away from the cameras

Hardly the most memorable film Jackman has ever made, but the interview plunges the reader right into the action and then sits down with the actor to explore the inner self. And we are immediately drawn into a contradiction – what you get is not always what you see; there's more to Hugh Jackman than bulging biceps. (His parents, it is revealed, were 'ten-pound Poms' – British citizens who paid to emigrate to Australia in the Sixties only for his mother to return to England, leaving her husband to bring up their five children).

Interviewing a demanding diva

When Marianne Macdonald came to interview a controversial opera singer for the *Evening Standard* magazine she chose to enter the lioness's den. The result is she captures the high-octane presence of a demanding diva whose life offstage is every bit as romantic and tragic as the roles she plays to perfection on stage:

The reader shares the writer's trepidation in awaiting the entrance of a notorious opera diva – and shares her relief when the star chooses to be positively kittenish. An unexpected change of mood makes for the promise of unexpected revelations

Waiting for Angela Gheorghiu in the bowels of the Royal Opera House is a nerve-racking ordeal. She is the world's most notorious opera diva, a woman whose tantrums leave Elton John squeaking in her majestic wake. She has a fearsome reputation for temperamental demands, reportedly insists on a make-up artist for a radio interview and once refused to wear a blonde wig at The Met until she was told: 'That wig is going on with or without you.' Then there are the perennial reports of cracks in her ten-year marriage to tenor Roberto Alagna with whom she fell in love on stage at Covent Garden; the couple were rechristened Bonnie and Clyde by the director Jonathan

Cascading hair, a
flashing diamond,
glossy lipstick and
a wicked grin – the
reader is face to face
with a notorious diva

Miller after he worked with them.

But when Angela finally appears, I am thankful to see that the legendary soprano is on her best behaviour; in fact, she's positively kittenish. At 41, she oozes sex (and indeed is said to insist on it before singing). Her thick hair falls down her shoulders like the Victoria Falls, diverted only by a pair of glossy black shades. Her rounded curves are outlined in an apple-green T-shirt and blue jeans, while a diamond ring shaped like a star flashes from her manicured hand. 'This is the ring from today!' she explains with a light laugh, as if to indicate the presence of numerous others. When I ask her what her perfect day is, she says: 'That depends. If I'm alone that's one thing. If I'm with Roberto it's different – oh la la! Et cetera, et cetera!' Then she gives a wicked grin and actually licks her glossed lips.

'Yes, I am a free spirit,' she says in her deep, heavily accented English, as if to imply it would be absurd to be otherwise.

The Royal Opera House was the natural location for an interview with Angela Gheorghiu and the reader will share Marianne Macdonald's sense of foreboding at confronting such an explosive reputation with her initial relief at that kittenish entrance. We tremble in anticipation, we witness the grand arrival, we listen to her deep, heavily accented voice; we are there.

Chaos in a serene suburban street

Consider now the opening of an interview by Rachel Cooke in the *Observer Magazine* of a controversial artist whose bustling canvases of London life include crowded markets, crime scenes – a blue plastic tape rattling in the breeze – and knots of young men arranged menacingly on street corners:

Artists, you might like to imagine, live in narrow Georgian houses (the rickety kind that look as thought they will topple like dominoes at any moment) or in vast warehouses, all light and space and bare floorboards. But not David Dawson. As my taxi pulls up outside his house, I worry that I have come to the wrong place, that an aproned housewife will open the door.

His home, which is deep in Kensal Rise, a determinedly down-at-heel corner of northwest London, lies at the end of an eerily serene cul-de-sac and dates from the Thirties. Pebble-dashed walls, red roof tiles, Velux windows, cherry trees … these things make me think not

Opening with a
description of an
ordinary scene can be
intriguing if what lies
beyond comes as a
surprise

of daring strokes of oil on canvas, but of the safe, the soporific – a round of golf, perhaps, or a gentle Sunday night sitcom.

'Yes, suburban, isn't it?' says Dawson, with a giggle. 'But I needed more room and this is what you can get in Kensal Rise for the price of a flat in Notting Hill.' Happily, inside, the chaos conforms more to the stereotype …

The kitchen is awash with dirty mugs and crumb-laden plates, the sitting room with newspapers, books and hastily scribbled notes. As for Dawson himself, he is a softly spoken creature with wispy grey hair and an expression of gentle surprise on his face. It is as though he is seeing everything, even his own home, for the first time.

A throwaway comment can help to interpret a subject's sense of values

Again, the intriguing element of contradiction. Openings which conjure up the unexpected strongly engage with readers, and run-down suburbia is an unlikely setting for an unconventional artist who was an assistant to Lucian Freud and is a friend of David Hockney. But Rachel Cooke goes further than that – not only providing a highly visual and atmospheric description of the modest home (in 'an eerily serene cul-de-sac') but using it to demonstrate Dawson's sense of values ('… this is what you can get in Kensal Rise for the price of a flat in Notting Hill').

In just four paragraphs we are well on the way to knowing what kind of person he really is. Which is exactly what an interview should set out to do.

Learning the lesson of homework

Having suggested that smart hotels and restaurants are not the most desirable of locations, there are ways to bring the occasion vividly to life. As in the piece by John Paul Flintoff for the *Sunday Times Magazine*:

The new James Bond arrives for lunch at the Dorchester Hotel. I'd half expected the screeching of brakes, or gunshots, but Daniel Craig arrives no more noisily than any other diner. He wears jeans, a black polo shirt that sets off his reddish tan and muscle-bound torso, and a thunderous expression that, combined with his unearthly, pale blue eyes, provides an air of authentic menace.

If I were one of Bond's enemies, I would lay a revolver on the table beside me. But I'm not, and Craig is no Bond. So I place on the table instead a well-thumbed copy of *A Number*, an intellectually

Potentially difficult interviews can be transformed when the writer reveals some surprising knowledge

Preparation is all-important. Questions that are obviously the result of prior research will win the confidence of the subject and make for a more revealing interview

challenging play by Caryl Churchill, in which Craig starred with Michael Gambon at London's Royal Court theatre in 2002, and for which he was nominated for an Evening Standard award. As soon as Craig sees it, his clenched jaws relax. He rolls his eyes, as if to say: 'Imagine bringing that old thing.'

It's a little contrived, but I had to do something. Craig hates publicity, and by the time we meet he has already endured almost a week of back-to-back junkets. I hate to think how many times he has been asked which Bond girl is his favourite, and which of his predecessors was the best James Bond. (He rolls his eyes. 'They're all great,' he answers to both.)

Not only an intriguing opening to the interview but an excellent example of the first rule of all celebrity interviews: **Do your homework!**

Hugh Grant's performance as a hapless *Horse and Hound* journalist interviewing the principals of a space movie in the film, *Notting Hill*, is an extreme example of the folly of ignorance. ('Are there any horses in the film?')

This sort of question is certain to doom any interview with someone entitled to feel they are a public figure. It not only irritates the subject and often brings the proceedings to an embarrassing halt, it betrays bad manners in displaying a total lack of professionalism. You are taking up the celebrity's precious time without having been prepared to spend your own time conducting the most basic research.

Conversely, the subject will often warm to the writer who can clearly demonstrate that he/she has done their homework. It certainly worked in the case of Daniel Craig, a star distasteful of the publicity grind of his business.

A bonus for breaking the rule

It is strongly recommended to start an interview by playing back to the subject the results of your research. This gives an opportunity for the interviewee to correct any inaccuracies in the public record and so wins his/her confidence. That makes it more likely to get honest answers to 'harder' questions later on in the interview.

A journalist who was prepared to risk dismissal in a bid to find a new way to freshen an old story

As a trainee feature writer in the 1960s, I valued that kind of lesson from a maverick freelance, Warwick Charlton, when he was commissioned to interview James Mason – a leading British actor who had achieved international stardom through a series of Hollywood roles. A ragingly intelligent man with a short temper, Mason viewed with contempt what he felt to be the unimaginative approach of the procession of journalists who had been sent to interview him over the years.

After making a visit to the magazine's library, Charlton could see why. In the days before digital archives, Mason's files occupied three drawers of a cabinet, each packed with cuttings stored in large brown folders. Leafing through them, he found only tired variations of a familiar storyline.

In total defiance of the office edict that no files should ever leave the building, Charlton seized the entire contents of all three drawers and carried them down a fire escape to reach an alleyway at the rear of the office from where he emerged to hail a taxi and proceed to the Savoy Hotel for the prearranged meeting with the reluctant star.

Told that a journalist was being sent up to his suite, Mason duly responded to the tap that came on his door – and blinked at what he saw. Standing there was a figure juggling to hold a 3ft-high pile of brown folders that reached more than head height. Then Charlton's beaming face emerged from behind the folders and a cheery voice announced: 'This is what everybody else has written about you over the years. We're both going to be wasting our time unless you are prepared to tell me something new!'

The ploy worked. Mason unburdened himself to a level no other interview had ever achieved. Charlton was reprimanded for stealing the files but received a bonus for what was generally regarded as an outstanding piece of copy.

What happened when a movie star opened the door and met a figure struggling behind a 3ft-high pile of brown folders?

Stating it, then proving it

James Silver of the *Guardian* had clearly done his homework on AA Gill, the colourfully provocative food and TV critic, before setting up the interview – establishing he took to drink at 15 and lived through two marriages by the time he was 30 and was packed off to a drying-out clinic after being warned his lifestyle would prove fatal; that he is so severely dyslexic he has to submit his copy by telephone.

And Silver actually welcomed Gill's suggestion of a neutral location. Where better to interview a food critic than in a posh restaurant?

It is mid-afternoon in the Wolseley, the stylish Piccadilly restaurant frequented by Prada-clad ladies who lunch and the kind of tourists who do not bat an eyelid at forking out £29.50 for a T-bone steak in Bearnaise sauce. Although lunchtime is over, the place is still packed and conversation booms around the high ceilings. AA Gill, the *Sunday Times*' long-serving restaurant and television critic, who

The special challenge when a journalist has to interview a journalist more famous than himself

asked me to meet him here as he was reviewing another restaurant nearby, strides towards the table, attracting a smattering of turned heads. The maitre d' and doorman aside, I'm not sure many recognize him. But he cuts the kind of C-list celebrity dash which makes people think they ought to know him.

Britain's most waspish and possibly best-paid critic is tanned, short-haired and handsome in a caddish, Merchant Ivory kind of way. You can imagine him in an EM Forster adaptation berating a butler or making overtures to someone else's wife. There is the touch of a dandy about him (he reportedly has his suit jackets lined with ladies' scarves and, later in our encounter, greets the doorman with a theatrical 'Darling'). He is notably trim for someone who claims to eat out six nights a week. On such a regimen, I'm sure the rest of use would have to be hoisted out of the bath.

He was, it turns out, impressed by the other restaurant. 'Actually it was very good,' he says, settling into his seat. 'Like every restaurant at the moment the food was a bit of everything: Indian, Malay, Thai, Singaporean – what I call Jabberwocky cooking. You read the menu and don't have the faintest idea of what any of it is.' But even though he has literally just left, he can't recall the restaurant's name. 'No idea, no it's gone, sorry.' Let us hope he remembers before he files his copy.

All the ingredients are there – Action (striding towards the table to cause a smattering of turned heads); Information (his job involves eating out six nights a week and he inhabits a world where a T-bone steak costs £29.50); Visual (his caddish good looks and dandyish clothes); and Sound (the boom of conversation in the restaurant and his quotes on Jabberwocky cooking and that self-confessed memory lapse).

James Silver also takes care to observe the rule that if you state it, prove it. To establish that this waspish critic provokes extreme reactions, the feature goes on to include anecdotes of Gill being threatened by a restaurateur who complained that a bad review had put him out of business, of being punched by Robert Kilroy-Smith for what he felt were unfair comments in a TV review and of being ejected by an irate Gordon Ramsay from one of his restaurants. Plus waspish quotes such as 'PR is the headlice of civilisation' ... 'The Apprentice is a freak show' ... 'Big Brother is 18-carat cant.'

It all adds up to a fully rounded picture of AA Gill.

Zooming in on a battered Greek god

Part of Cole Moreton's interview with the then England rugby captain for the *Mail on Sunday's Live Magazine* was having a lift in his car. Not exactly a gripping setting for a battle-hardened sporting warrior so he decided to make the principal location of the feature his subject's face – zooming in on a battered Greek god.

> There's a blur where the bridge of Lewis Moody's nose should be. Just an empty space. The England rugby star also has a woozy eye, cuts and scratches on both cheeks and scars on his forehead, under wild, straw hair. He's powerfully built, of course, like a Greek god – but one whose statue has been bashed about a bit. Just how many knocks has this man taken for his sport? Oh dear. That's vast. Let's think.
>
> 'I've had two broken noses, a fractured cheek, three shoulder reconstructions and a hip micro-fracture, a broken hand, a fractured navicular bone in the right foot, an Achilles rupture, a broken toe … three broken toes, actually. God, it's been endless.
>
> 'These are the only ones I can remember. I know I've had 11 operations in 15 seasons, not including relatively minor injuries like muscle tears that keep you out for a few weeks. And I've damaged my retina, so I will never have complete vision in my left eye again.'
>
> And then, of course, there's that wretched twisted knee, which sidelined him during the first part of the Six Nations campaign. But he's on his way back now, and should captain England through the World Cup in New Zealand in the summer. He's certainly missed. 'Every time I play with him, he's an inspiration,' says England wing Mark Cueto. 'He always puts his body on the line. If you told him to stand in front of a train, he's do it.'
>
> For proof of that, look online to see how Moody injured his eye back in October. He threw himself headlong on to the boot of an opposing fullback, to charge down a kick. No wonder they call him Mad Dog.

Cole Moreton not only produces a highly visual opening but gets Moody to list his medical history for the reader, switches to the testimony of a teammate and sets up an action shot of his latest injury. What better introduction to a seriously mad sportsman?

Of course, not every interview is with a celebrity and the less well-known the subjects the more important the location. By choosing to place them in their relevant settings and so creating a backcloth to

When the physical setting for an interview is far from dramatic the writer must turn to other ways of creating a powerful intro

A contribution from an old friend or colleague provides an extra dimension to an interview

The location of celebrity interviews is difficult to control. But for 'more ordinary' subjects, the writer should seek to place them in locations which define their identity. That will immediately make them less ordinary

their lives, your description can go wide-screen instead of presenting just a talking head.

Create a backcloth to their lives

Where better to interview an offshore fisherman than on his boat? If not at sea then at the quayside when unloading his latest catch – his words punctuated by the shrieks of hovering seagulls and the trundling of rusty winches, the brine still fresh upon his beard, his clothes carrying the stale stench of long-departed fish.

Where better to interview an old boxer than in the gymnasium he now runs? Fading posters of him in his prime, the contrast between his battered features and the shining eyes of his young hopefuls, the persistent rhythm of thuds against punchbags, the smell of sweat and embrocations.

Where better to interview a long-distance lorry driver than riding with him in his cab? Or a headmistress in the playground of her troublesome inner-city school rather than in her study? Or a racehorse trainer on the morning gallops?

Look as well as listen

Location interviews depend heavily on the degree of observation deployed, the ability to project the whole scene instead of merely recording and recycling the words of the subject.

Three different business journals sent feature writers to record the success story of the self-made millionaire chief of a haulage company celebrating its 25th anniversary.

The location was not promising – the first-floor office at his headquarters in an industrial backwater – and was lost upon the first visitor who duly established the rags-to-riches story and went back to produced a verbatim account of what was said.

The second journalist was more observant. He caught the moment when his subject sprang from his seat behind an intimidating desk, walked over to the window, gestured below and said 'See that yard down there? When I started, I had two lorries; now I have one of the largest fleets in the country and they queue for half an hour at a time to get in and out.' For the rest of the interview he prowled restlessly around the office, finally explaining: 'I just envy those drivers down there. Here I am, stuck behind a desk all day when I would love to be out and about as one of the lads again – sitting behind the wheel of a 10-tonner beating up the Great North Road.'

There's animation and passion in that story. How much more revealing of a working man made good?

The third visiting journalist – perhaps, significantly, female – crisply established the facts and figures of his remarkable career while noting that this reputedly ruthless operator had the framed portrait of wife and two children on the corner of the desk next to a Dinky toy lorry, and had an autographed picture of one of Liverpool FC's Champions League winning teams hanging on the wall.

Secret from the rest of the industry

She also thought to enquire after the large tank of tropical fish mounted above his desk, illuminated from behind to send swirling shadows around the room as the exotic creatures swam to and fro. Which produced the explanation that, unknown to the rest of the industry, a cash-flow crisis in the 1990s had brought the company close to bankruptcy and he had suffered a nervous breakdown.

'The worst part was that I just couldn't sleep at night, tossing and turning and worrying what was going to happen. Then a psychiatrist suggested I had this sort of fish tank installed in my bedroom with the light behind it left on all night. It was utterly fascinating to lie in bed and watch the shadowy patterns endlessly changing across the ceiling as the fish gently twisted and turned and I found I was falling asleep in no time. The whole effect was so relaxing that when I was better I had this tank put in my office and I've never had a business worry since.'

Who produced the best story? Who produced the most engrossing picture of a vulnerable man the rest of the world saw as Mr Success?

Even an industrial office can be a revealing location if the writer will only look as well as listen.

Creating action from within

But, very often, a feature is assembled by way of interviews and research across a range of locations, none of which provides a highly visual, all-action setting for the opening. The solution is to borrow a location from within the content of the story and open with an anecdote that provides the requisite note of arresting drama.

Interviewing is not merely the recording of the spoken word. It is an exercise in the art of observation. Whether noting a sudden change of body language at the mention of a certain topic, spotting the prominence of a faded family photograph or managing a quick appraisal of the contents of a bookshelf – these all may provide clues to the real person

If there is no alternative to conducting an interview in the nearest coffee bar or pub, an anecdote plucked from the heart of the story can provide a dramatic opening in a most colourful setting

The consistent use of anecdotes as a dramatic way to open its stories produced the world's most successful magazine

This is the technique perfected by *Reader's Digest* in the course of its reign as the one-time world's largest circulation magazine. See how Mary Fisher opened her story of a stalker's victim:

> On a spring day in 2004, Gayane Indzheyan was sitting outside a Starbucks café in a busy shopping centre near her home. The café was part of a bookshop bustling with the usual browsers, groups of students and people writing on laptops or reading novels. Book buyers and coffee drinkers came and went. A normal day. Then Gayane happened to glance up and noticed a man peering at her from the crowded car park. He stared at her with a strange intensity – their eyes met and then he was gone …

In one paragraph, the writer gives a peaceful suburban scene a hint of menace. A fellow *Digest* contributor, Declan Walsh, chose a much more turbulent setting for the intro to a feature on forced marriages in Pakistan:

> Yasmin Rehman darts through the sleepy Punjabi village. Running down a sandy lane, the 21-year-old from the north of England, heads for the main road, her green *salwar kameez* streaming in her wake. Behind her, clutching a hastily packed suitcase, is British diplomat Jon Turner, at his side a Pakistani bodyguard, a pistol concealed under his clothes.
>
> A Land Rover is waiting at the end of the lane. Yasmin and her escort leap in and it roars off, weaving around donkeys, tractors and a gaggle of curious kids.
>
> Yasmin had just escaped a nightmare: she had been beaten, threatened at gunpoint and forced to marry a complete stranger. 'I can't trust my family, never again,' she says in her strong northern accent. 'Next time they could kill me.'
>
> Such is the plight of dual nationals caught in forced marriages in Pakistan that a special team has been established inside the British High Commission in Islamabad to rescue them. Last year the team saved 108 young people …

Description of three figures running down a crowded street can lead into a story of high drama

A truly cinematic opening providing all the necessary ingredients – Action (the girl fleeing, the car weaving through the traffic), Information (she's one of 108 to be rescued), Visuals (the street scene, the green garment streaming behind her) and Sounds (she speaks with a northern accent).

The *Digest* approach serves well for that staple of many magazines:

the true-life drama. Ruth Addicott provides a typical example:

> A huge wave crashed on Rob Starr's head, sending him spinning out of control. The 44-year-old's plan had been to squeeze in an early morning training swim along Brighton beach to the Palace Pier, but the weather had turned and he'd been swept out by the tide.
>
> He knew he had to get back to the shore as quickly as possible, but the waves were not only dragging him under, but also pulling him closer and closer to the pier's sharp metal stanchions. He was at serious risk of being torn to shreds.
>
> 'My heart was going a hundred to the dozen,' he remembers now. 'I literally closed my eyes, and was picked up by a wave, shot under the pier and thrown on to the pebbles. My trunks were torn off and I was covered in cuts. But I was OK.' …

The big value of the anecdotal intro is that it creates an immediate involvement with the central character of the story

That was the intro to the story of a middle-aged man with a chronic medical history ('You have the spine of a 96-year-old,' his doctor warned him) who decides to swim the English Channel to raise money for charity.

Open with your most exciting anecdote

But the approach works at any level. If set to interview a local paramedic, open with his most exciting anecdote – the night he rescued a badly injured security guard from the basement of a blazing factory. That way, the reader can't wait to find out more about him. If an ex-convict-turned-social-worker, have him standing in the dock hearing he was to go to prison for a long time and then switch to the moment of redemption which led to his becoming a pillar of the local community.

When John Preston went to write about tennis star Roger Federer for the *Sunday Telegraph Magazine* the interview took place amid rows and rows of empty seats in a deserted press centre at the end of a long concrete corridor.

Yet he was able to give his opening the colourful location of an international sports stadium simmering with excitement at the start of a big tournament and by telling the story of a schoolboy fan emerging from an adoring crowd and, not content with landing Federer's autograph, cheekily asking to be given his shirt as well. The normally flamboyant Federer shrugs apologetically and says: 'I'm sorry, but I need my stuff.'

A small boy emerging from a crowded stadium can be the unlikely peg for a revealing interview

A list of negatives can add up to a positive assessment of a complex personality

Which makes a perfect opening peg for Preston to go on to write: 'These days, everyone wants a piece of Roger Federer' – and for him to devote the next several hundred words explaining just why.

Another reason why a sense of location gives an interview an extra dimension.

The art of topping and tailing

Mary Riddell's interview with George Melly for the *Daily Mail's Weekend* magazine was most satisfyingly packaged in that it had an arresting opening mirrored by a poignant final paragraph. She wrote:

> George Melly is not one for gadgets. He has never learned to work a video recorder, and the thought of carrying a mobile phone appals him. 'My wife says: "But what if you collapse when you are out fishing? No one might find you for hours." I tell her that I'd much rather die by the river bank than in hospital.'
>
> For a man nicknamed Good-time George, who has lived flamboyantly for 77 years, a final exit lacking in panache would be unthinkable.

After chronicling a life of wild excesses, heavy drinking and bisexual escapades Mary concludes:

> His hearing is poor, his vision hazy and the afflictions of old age crowd in on him. George, who loves his life and has no fear of death, smiles wryly and says brightly: 'Getting old is terrible, you keep telling people the same anecdotes.'
>
> That doughty cheerfulness defines George Melly's charm and saving grace. He may have too little sympathy for others, but he reserves even less pity for himself.

6 Breathing Life into Hard Facts

The Hallmarking exercise demonstrates how successful factual features also embrace the four elements of VISA. Producing a 3,300-word feature for the lay audience of the *Telegraph Magazine* on an obscure medical condition – body dysmorphic disorder – Sally Williams duly assembled the four key ingredients:

Sufferers of body dysmorphic disorder see only distorted and grotesque versions of themselves in the mirror; the condition affects one in 100 people. **So why are diagnosis and treatment so difficult to get?** Sally Williams meets a family whose lives were turned upside down by the illness. Illustrations by Wesley Allsbrook

Samantha Davies was 13 when she began to develop the deformities that would transform her into what she described as 'the most ugly person in the world'. Her nose began to spread into a formless lump across her face, her cheeks inflated to three times their normal size and her head became square and masculine.

First, she tried hiding behind make-up. She would use so much foundation that 'her face was just orange, like a mask', her mother says. She would apply six or seven layers of mascara. She would straighten her hair (to cover her face) with hair irons to the point of singeing it.

After three months she decided ... too monstrous to be seen. She confined herself to her ... and refused to go to school. She would agree to be taught ... only if the tutor couldn't see her face. 'She would sit on the bed with a quilt over her head. The woman would teach her through the quilt,' her mother remembers. Finally, aged 13 and a half, Samantha had enough. She took an overdose. And if this wasn't evidence enough of her state of mind at that point, her reaction when she came to in hospital underlined it. 'My first thought was, "What do I look like?" And the feelings of self-revulsion returned.

At her worst, Samantha was checking her face in the mirror 80 times a day, sometimes for up to two hours at a time

The strange thing is that Samantha looks perfectly normal. It was all in her head. In October 2009, after months of anguish and ... de attempts, she was finally treated for sever ... smorphic disorder. Body dysmorphic disorder ... is driven by intense anxiety about appearance ... in its delusional quality. The focus can be any body part, but typically it is the head – hair, nose, ears, skin, the size and shape of the jaw – which sufferers see as ugly, 'not right'.

'I remember a colleague from the States who was treating a soldier in the American Army. He had ... he front line in Iraq and had been shot at and all he ... about was the size of his nose; that is how intense ... ing the preoccupation can be,' says Dr David Matai ... fessor and consultant clinical psychologist at the Institute of Psychiatry and at the Maudsley Hospital, London, which has ramped up its service for young people with BDD in the past year.

BDD is relatively common – it affects about one in 100 people (significantly more than schiz ... slightly more than anorexia). It typically starts in ... affects boys as frequently as girls. The causes of BD ... nknown. 'We know it runs in families and that there is ... genetic component, but that doesn't explain the whole picture,' Dr Matais-Cols says, listing such factors as 'appearance-related teasing' and bullying. 'It's not clear if they simply trigger a pre-existing vulnerability, or

Action

Sufferers see only grotesque versions of themselves when they look in the mirror. We are able to watch one patient (a Welsh teenager, Samantha Davies) looking in the mirror and to capture her thoughts on what she sees ... We witness her chopping off her shoulder-length hair in disgust at the face before her ... We can picture her hanging her dressing-gown cord from a tree in preparation for one of three suicide attempts ... We see her mother pleading for financial help from the Welsh Assembly.

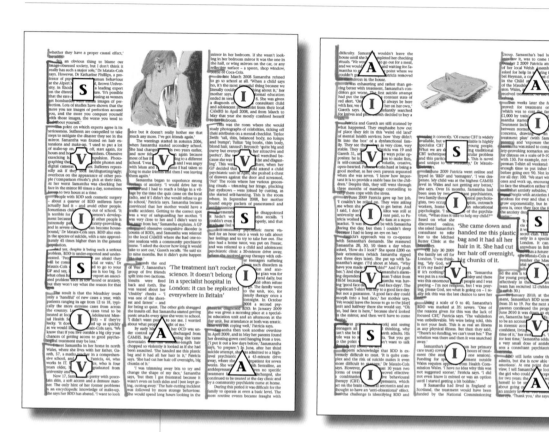

Information

The causes of body dysmorphic disorder (BDD) are lucidly defined: we learn it affects more people than schizophrenia and anorexia and affects boys as much as girls, that the suicide rate is 45 times higher than in the general population, that country dwellers are less likely to receive proper treatment – which can impose a heavy financial burden. Williams lists the procedures undergone by the sufferer as she is seen by two consultant psychiatrists, two family therapists, two clinical psychologists, two occupational therapists, outreach workers, home tutors and an educational psychologist. A combination of cognitive behavioural therapy (known as CBT) and antidepressants is being hailed as offering a solution to the problem but the writer makes clear that BDD is not always properly identified.

Visuals

Now 17, Samantha is introduced as 'pretty with porcelain skin, a soft accent and a demure manner' – yet needing reassurance from her mother 50 times a day that she was not 'just plain and fat and disgusting.' We meet her parents and elder sister, hear of her troubled schooldays, visit the bedroom where her various grooming rituals – trimming her fringe, plucking her eyebrows – were joined by cutting as she started self-harming and consuming packets of paracetamol and antihistamines. The feature tells how her mother ('I'm not religious') was driven to prayer before Samantha agreed to undertake a course of 14 individualized treatments that have finally abated her 'excessive appearance concerns.'

Sounds

The voice of the obsessive teenager is little heard in the piece. Of her first suicide attempt she says: 'I remember being quite disappointed it hadn't worked. I couldn't even kill myself properly, and that made me feel worse.' But there are plenty of revealing quotes from her parents (driven to remove all the mirrors in the house) on the frustration and anguish of being unable to help their tormented child. And the two specialists principally concerned with the case provide an expert commentary on her progress

Interweaving the four ingredients

The Hallmarking breakdown of the finished feature shows how deftly Sally interwove those four ingredients so that no one element was projected to any great length without being balanced by a change of pace or mood. She provides a fitting conclusion. The feature opened with Samantha convinced she is the ugliest girl in the world – seeing her nose spread into a formless lump across her face, her cheeks inflated to three times their normal size and her head square and masculine. At the end of the final interview, Sally chooses to tell Samantha how lovely she really is and the girl who could never accept compliments and lived in fear of 'bad face' days looks the writer in the eye and says 'Thank you.' And smiles.

'You've got a right good one there'

Similarly, when Clover Hughes attended a horse fair in the Cotswolds the result could have been a piece of mundane reportage for *Horse and Hound*. Instead, she brought the occasion to life with another well-structured feature for the *Telegraph Magazine*:

Information clearly plays a dominant role in factual features but still needs to be balanced by the human interest created by elements of Visuals, Action and Sounds

'Mind yer backs,' shouts the gipsy with a thick Irish accent standing behind me. He has wild, dark eyes, and on each of his middle fingers is a heavy gold sovereign ring. His greasy pin-stripe suit is straining around his wide frame, the mismatched buttons popping off their threads. A greyhound lying at his feet shivers in the sharp October sunlight. Down at the bottom of the muddy field I can hear hard male voices shouting to each other in a heavily accented mix of English and Romany that I cannot understand. Two younger gipsies race their trotting ponies in low-slung carts up the edge of the field. I drag my buggy out of the way as the ponies thunder past with a flash of shiny silver harness and a wink from one of the boys on the cart. My two-year-old son Jimmy Joe shrieks with excitement. As if he has only just noticed him, the gipsy looks down and smiles, revealing a mouthful of gold teeth.

'He's a game little piece of gear, lady,' he says. 'You've got a right good one there.'

Clover has thus laced together Visuals ('wild, dark eyes' ... 'greasy pin-striped suit' ... 'mouthful of gold teeth'); Sounds (English and Romany voices shouting to each other, her son shrieking with excitement); Action (ponies thundering past with a flash of silver harness – even buttons popping off their threads).

Information there is in plenty as the story progresses – how the fair was founded by royal charter in 1476; how Daniel Defoe was a visitor before he wrote *Robinson Crusoe* and noted 20,000 sheep changing hands; how it became a horse fair when the wool trade declined; how the estimated 200,000 gipsies and travellers in the United Kingdom resent that the Criminal Justice Act of 1994 repealed local councils' statutory duty to provide sites for gipsies.

But facts are interspersed with evocative passages such as:

An evocative style not only captures all the atmosphere of the horse fair but delivers a history lesson as well

I leave the field, full of gipsy men conducting lengthy and subtle horse deals with each other and the rows of horseboxes that have spilled their cargoes of black-and-white ponies out into the mud, and walk back down the road. The narrow verge is lined with stalls selling harnesses, cooking pots and cast-iron kettles, grand old prams, blankets patterned with roses and animal prints, canaries in delicate wooden cages, gaudy satin baby clothes and kitsch china decorated with pictures of ponies. Parked between the stalls are white trailers, but there are horse-drawn wagons too, as dazzling as a clutch of Fabergé eggs.

Moving around the fair, Clover captures the smells of hot dogs and fried onions mixed with wood smoke. She introduces a personal anecdote in recounting how as a child cycling past a gipsy camp on the way to school she became 'glassy-eyed with envy at the dark-haired girls who ran free, unencumbered by school bags and spelling tests.' Such was the romantic appeal of such a life, she reveals that her first proper boyfriend was a traveller.

The writer's ability to introduce a personal anecdote demonstrates her feeling for the subject

Joining an Irish mother of ten children as she cooks a freshly skinned hare over an open fire, Clover records her saying:

> 'I can't read or write but I would like my grandchildren to be educated. In most cases the councils make that very hard. If we park up we mostly get moved on, even if there is a new baby in the camp or an old person sick. This life is getting harder, there's no doubt of that. We're like wild birds in a cage.'

Who would have thought a horse fair could be so revealing?

Reflecting the balance of the story

The four ingredients of VISA do not have to be in equal measure. Their respective weights will depend on the nature of the story. Some features will be more descriptive than others, some more reflective, some more conversational.

For example, any Hallmarking of William Langewiesche's 9,000-word examination of the causes of the Columbia space shuttle disaster for the *Observer Magazine* would have had much of its 10 pages dominated by (I) and S because this was necessarily Information-heavy (much of it technical). A lot of the dialogue concerned space engineering.

But, even with this kind of topic, it demonstrates that there are opportunities to bring situations to life.

Hal Geham, the retired four-star admiral appointed to chair the inquiry into the disaster, is not left as just another name among the many admirals, generals and aviation experts listed as being involved in the proceedings. We come to see him:

Facts and figures are bound to dominate a largely technical subject but there is always room for the human touch

> 'At the age of 60, Gehman was a tall, slim, silver-haired man with an unlined face and soft eyes ... standing straight but not stiffly so, he had an accessible, unassuming manner that contrasted with the rank and power he had achieved.'

The home life of a
retired admiral and his
secret passion reveal
him as more than just
another name in the
cast list

So that's what he looked like. But what sort of man was he?

> 'He lived in Norfolk in a pleasant house that he had recently
> remodelled: loved his wife, his grown children, his mother and father,
> and all his siblings. He had an old Volkswagen bug convertible,
> robin's-egg blue.'

What an inspired piece of information. How many retired admirals are
do-it-yourself enthusiasts to be seen driving around in an old Beetle
coloured robin's-egg blue?

Delivering the final report

We come to witness the moment of Gehman actually delivering the
official copy of his final report to Nasa's administrator, Sean O'Keefe:
Travelling to Nasa headquarters in a car driven by a Navy officer
in whites (a neat contrast to that exotically coloured Volkswagen)
Gehman and an aide

> 'strode up the carpeted hallways in a phalanx of anxious, dark-suited
> Nasa staffers, who swung open the doors in advance and followed
> close on their heels. O'Keefe's office suite was practically imperial
> in its expense and splendour. High officials stood in small, nervous
> groups, murmuring. After a short delay O'Keefe appeared – a tall,
> balding, gray-haired man with stooped shoulders...'

A mother's lament

We can see the procession of anxious staffers, hear the nervous
murmurs of high officials and when we reach O'Keefe's luxurious
office a pen-picture of just nine words turns a name into a
recognizable human being.

Another human touch is recording a mother lamenting 'Those damn
kids' after a piece of debris from the disintegrating space shuttle ripped
open the backyard trampoline. Other debris 'whistled down through
the leaves of trees and smacked into a pond where a man was fishing'.

Note that the debris didn't just fall; it 'whistled' and 'smacked'.
Recording sounds is very much part of creative writing.

Glimpses of the apparently inconsequential can lift the most serious
tract. We learn that in the search across thousands of square miles

Official reports on
major inquiries are
duly submitted and its
findings recorded. The
writer achieves a note
of drama by describing
the actual moment of
the document being
delivered

of snake-infested brushland for clues to the disaster the investigators came across plenty of junked cars, clandestine meth labs – and the remains of several apparent murder victims.

More significantly, among the wreckage recovered was a home movie shot on board as the shuttle was re-entering the earth's atmosphere. The crew are heard chatting like sightseers as sheets of fiery plasma began to pass by the windows, turning bright orange-yellow over the nose. 'It's really neat,' says one. 'Amazing,' says another. 'Wow,' says a third.

Seconds later the shuttle disintegrated at nearly 17,000 mph.

Across the 9,000 words examining the intricate mechanics of the disaster, Langewiesche has made sure that the reader is never far away from the people at the heart of the story.

It is a rule documentary feature writers should strive to observe.

Within a 9,000-word piece on a heavily technical subject, the creative feature writer can still provide vivid glimpses of the human drama at the heart of the matter

7 You've Gotta Have Style

Observing the basic mechanics of the construction of a feature – ensuring a well-balanced mixture of **Visuals, Information, Sounds** and **Actions** – will provide a fluent flow of words. Whether they will prove memorable depends on the ability to infuse them with **Style**

Style is what lifts writing from merely the assembling of words into a coherent sequence to creating a distinctive tone of voice that expresses the personality of the writer.

The mood may be provocative or flippant, earnest or cool, whimsical or clinical, but the flavour will linger. And the writer who establishes a recognizable personal Style will generate a committed following among the reading public.

Since the most compelling Style is highly personal there can be no elementary guide to achieving this vital element. But if we are using words to paint pictures then stand back from your easel and decide what sort of pictures you want to create.

Daily Telegraph columnist Zoe Strimpel spells out the challenge:

> As soon as I was old enough to hold a pen, I'd grab one wherever possible and start scrawling; on bank slips, newspapers – whatever. Since then, my intellectual and emotional universe has been defined not by logic, art or numbers, but by words – spoken, written, imagined, felt. Yet words – intensely interesting to their creators – can be boring, mystifying, meaningless and even sinister to others. And with the daily tsunami of digital content we face today, never has choosing them wisely mattered more. Yet to write well, to choose words with intelligence, is hard. Sometimes it's very hard, like lifting stubbornly heavy weights in the gym. But it's the best kind of hard work, and it's essential – nothing less will do…
>
> It's also a pleasure, because when you have sweated enough over your piece, clarified your thoughts, sometimes rearranging the whole thing over a single word or phrase, your work finally sings, like a violin sonata being played in tune. This is our job and the readers deserve nothing less.

If the same rural landscape can produce vastly different views from generations of painters so can a writer bring familiar situations to new life by the kind of imagery he chooses to employ.

One way is to employ words that in themselves readily conjure up images.

In the early days of the talkies, a New York copywriter tried to break into Hollywood by convincing studio executives that he commanded all the words their scripts would ever need. In a letter of application, Robert Pirosh wrote:

> 'I like words. I like buttery words, such as ooze, turpitude, glutinous, toady. I like solemn angular, creaky words such as straight-laced, cantankerous, pecunious, valedictory. I like spurious, black-is-white words, such as mortician, liquidate, tonsorial, demi-monde. I like suave 'V' words, such as Svengali, svelte, bravura, verve. I like crunchy, brittle, crackly words, such as splinter, grapple, jostle, crusty. I like sullen, crabbed, scowling words, such as skulk, glower, scabby, churl … I like wormy, squirmy, mealy words, such as crawl, blubber, squeal, drip. I like sniggly, chuckling words, such as cowlick, gurgle, bubble and burp.'

These are words communicating movement (to ooze, to skulk, to jostle, to grapple, to crawl, to bubble), mood (to scowl, to glower, crusty), manner (glutinous, toady, svelte),sounds (blubber, squeal, gurgle and burp).

They are words that immediately alert your senses, each one flashing a distinctive image to your mind. You don't just read the word 'ooze' you see it oozing.

In all, not a bad vocabulary for a man wanting to marry words with images on the silver screen and his letter worked to the extent that Robert Pirosh went on to win an Oscar and Golden Globe during a 15-year career in Hollywood.

Another way to achieve style is by way of analogy, largely expressed through similes and metaphor – the first describing a courageous man as brave as a lion, the second saying he is lion-hearted. Courageous is just a statement, nothing to see except the word on the page; the other two descriptions bring a noble animal into the mind.

When a humorist takes a bus ride

A master of this technique is Bill Bryson, a former newspaper sub-editor, now an internationally best-selling author, largely of humorous travel books. Here is how he can turn a bus ride into sheer entertainment:

> The bus was a large double-decker, **like an American Greyhound,**

Individual words are more than able to provides sounds and pictures in the reader's mind

An adjective can be little more than a word on a page. Similes and metaphors create images which capture the imagination

covered with a worryingly psychedelic painting of an intergalactic landscape, like the cover of a pulp science-fiction novel.

I quickly realised that everything about the bus was designed for discomfort, so that while chill draughts teased my upper extremities, my left leg grew **so hot I could hear the hairs on it crackle.**

The seats were designed by **a dwarf seeking revenge on full-sized people**; there was no other explanation.

The young man in front of me put his seat so far back that his head was all but in my lap. He was reading a comic book and had the sort of face that **makes you realise God does have a sense of humour.**

The analogies get even more fanciful when Bryson takes to the air:

Everyone on the transatlantic was a hippie, except the crew and two herring-factory executives in first class. It was rather **like being on a Greyhound bus on the way to a folk-singers' convention.** People were forever pulling out guitars and mandolins and bottles of Thunderbird wine.

In the long, exciting weeks preceding the flight I had sustained myself with a series of **bedroom ceiling fantasies** that generally involved finding myself seated next to a panting young beauty being sent by her father to the Lausanne Institute for Nymphomaniacal Disorders, who would turn to me somewhere over mid-Atlantic and say: 'Forgive me, but would it be all right if I sat on your face for a while?'

In the event my seatmate turned out to be an acned streambean with **Buddy Holly glasses.** He had boils on his neck which looked **like bullet wounds that had never quite healed** and smelled oppressively of Vicks VapoRub.

I spent the flight secretly watching out of the window for Europe. I still remember that first sight.

The plane dropped out of the clouds and there below me was this magical tableau of small green fields and **steepled villages** spread across an undulating landscape, **like a shaken-out quilt just settling back on a bed.**

I had flown a lot in America and never seen much from an aeroplane window but endless golden fields on farms **the size of Belgium,** meandering rivers and **pencil lines of black highways as straight as taut wire**. But here the landscape had the **ordered perfection of a model railway layout.**

It was all so green and minutely cultivated, so compact, so tidy, so fetching so … European. I was smitten. I still am.

Bill Bryson has the ability to make the reader feel they are sitting next to him, looking out the same aircraft window

Picture the scene-setting conjured up by another American writer, Laura Hillenbrand, in her book on Seabiscuit, the legendary racehorse:

Someone simply entering a room can become a colourful vision if a writer has style

> Charles Howard had the feel of **a gigantic onrushing machine**; you had to either climb or leap out of the way. He would sweep into a room, working a cigarette in his fingers, and people would trail him **like pilot fish**. They couldn't help themselves. Fifty-eight years old in 1935, Howard was a tall, glowing man in a big suit and drove a very big Buick. But it wasn't his physical bearing that did it.
>
> He lived on a Californian ranch **so huge that a man could take a wrong turn on it and be lost forever**, but it wasn't his circumstances either. Nor was it that he spoke out loud and long; the surprise of this man was his understatement, the quiet and kindly intimacy of his acquaintance.
>
> On an afternoon in 1903, long before the big cars and the ranch and all the money, Howard began his adulthood with only that air of destiny and 21 cents in his pocket. He sat in the **swaying belly** of a transcontinental train, **snaking west** from New York. He was 26, handsome, gentlemanly, with a bounding imagination. Back then he had more hair than anyone who knew him later would have guessed. He was eastern born and bred but he had **the restlessness of a westerner**.

See how vividly Jane Shilling, columnist with *The Times*, projects a word-picture of an English country house:

> In my late 30s, I formed an attachment to a man who **collected houses and land in the way that some other people collect furniture or stamps or first editions**. Far to the north, this man had a huge, hideous, comfortable, square Victorian shooting lodge in which everything was built on a slightly greater than human scale.
>
> The taps of the **coffin-shaped bath** gushed with a tide of what **looked like boiling tea**. The bath itself was like **an exceptionally roomy sarcophagus**; so capacious that when you got in, you had to cling to the taps with your toes to avoid floating away. In the bedroom, a curtained bed was **moored on a calm sea of carpet; a galleon at anchor in a harbour bobbing with smaller craft** – standing mirrors and chests of drawers artistically painted with blue bows and wreaths of pink rosebuds. From the window was a **view as pure as cold water**; a pale arc of sky, the rising swell of a hill, an expanse of flat, cropped lawn on which, waking one morning at dawn, I found a herd of deer, branchy heads bent towards dewed grass, **still as the moment before some mythic catastrophe**.

AA Gill was so chronically dyslexic that he had to dictate his copy but the words flowed smoothly

Waxing lyrical over a beach café

A very different style (very much his own) is employed by AA Gill to give *Sunday Times* readers his quirky view of the English seaside:

> The beach: a place that ebbs and flows in retrospect. Children who aren't given seaside summers are more deprived than **if they'd been forbidden television, pets or narcotic suppositories**. For the English, the annual fortnight by the coast is as rich in cliché-bonding as the sweets of your baby teeth and your first Blue Peter presenter, more important than GCSEs, polio inoculations, dentistry or a roof.
>
> The sea is central to this island's story; not literally central obviously, because that would make it a lake, but peripheral in a symbolically centrist sense. Actually, it's not so much the sea as the beach. The sea is a step too far. Look out to sea on a summer holiday and you think: **'Bugger me, that's cold enough to geld a furry donkey.'** But the beach is where you go to look out on the broad horizons of possibility and see that **the world is your cockle** – even if **it's so windy out there, it could sandblast the wrinkles off a pensioner's scrotum.**
>
> We all look back on seaside holidays **with a heightened, messianic reverie**. The them and us of this island is not between indigenous and immigrant, black and white, Muslim and football, but between those of us who, as children, went to the seaside and ate mangoes and grilled parrotfish, swam in the warm surf, collected seashells and watched glorious sunsets and those who went to the seaside, hugged their knees and yomped with damp sand in their socks across muddy strands, carrying plastic bags full of sodden towels and **grit-battered jam sandwiches**.

A mixture of nostalgia, social history, humour, indiscreet language and a lyrical sentence 81 words long – all so typical of AA Gill. And it was only the opening to his review of the food in a beach café in Dorset.

Return of the Messiah

See how sports writer Barney Ronay brings to life Jose Mourinho's first press conference on returning to Chelsea Football Club three years after being sacked as manager:

> The first sighting of the man himself brought an **audible gurgle of pleasure.**

There he was at the front of the stage in a surprisingly shiny black body-warmer, the irresistible smile and the air of natural celebrity still thrillingly intact. He stopped to embrace a white-haired old man; you **half-expected him to rise up and throw away his crutches** rather than merely offer his scarf for an autograph ...

The English press always loved Mourinho. Right from the start they swooned and gushed as he fed them lines: no filler, just ready-loaded, perfectly pitched **wise-guy gobbets.** At his first Chelsea press conference Mourinho had looked **like a time-traveller**, a managerial format update, not to mention the **bastardishly handsome Mafioso business tycoon in a Mediterranean daytime soap opera**. Six years of elite management have taken their toll very slightly. Mourinho is still ferrety and slender. He now **has the face of a slightly worn but still precocious boy prodigy**. The silky hair has atrophied a little into a greying bouffant. **Previously he had pin-up hair. This is being replaced by something more substantial: senior diva hair, Hollywood hair, Liz Taylor hair.**

Economy can be effective

The writers quoted have clearly revelled in the richness of the imagery they have been able to conjure up but more sparing use of analogy can be strikingly effective.

Ernest Hemingway, that arch exponent of staccato dialogue and terse prose, allows one of his characters in a story of a journey across Spain to say of a sprawl of sunlit hills beyond a brown and dry landscape: 'They look like white elephants' (a vivid phrase I have remembered ever since driving through the same valley half a century ago).

Hemingway's use of analogy tended to be laconic:
- A beautiful woman 'was built with the curves of a racing yacht'
- A Spanish peasant's legs were 'tanned the colour of saddle leather'
- The ball of smoke from a rocket 'hung in the sky like a shrapnel burst'
- A packed crowd 'moved slowly as a glacier'
- The spoken language of the English upper classes 'has fewer words than the Eskimo'

Even the fiercely disciplined Hemingway could allow himself to be more expansive. The doomed hero of his novel, *For Whom the Bells Toll*, contemplates his fate as his enemies close in for the kill:

The briefest of phrases can help to create vivid pictures in the mind

Sporting journalism is notoriously riddled with clichés yet offers rich opportunities for genuine style

Dying was nothing and he had no picture of it nor fear of it in his mind. But living was a field of grain blowing in the wind on the side of a hill. Living was a hawk in the sky. Living was an earthen jar of water in the dust of the threshing with the grain flailed out. Living was a horse between your legs and a carbine under one leg and a hill and a valley and a stream with trees along it and the far side of the valley and the hills beyond.

Words that pictured the fevered mind of a man about to die. A fictional situation created by a famous novelist, yet on the real-life occasion of Mourinho's return to Chelsea Football Club journalist Barney Ronay might claim to have been equally imaginative in suggesting the white-haired old man embraced by his hero might rise and throw away his crutches instead of merely wanting his scarf autographed or that the extrovert manager resembled a Mafioso business tycoon in a Mediterranean soap opera.

Sports reporting is notoriously riddled with clichés. The images Ronay produces are freshly minted.

Phrases that enter the language

Although the occasional well-worn but apposite cliché is not to be scorned (and remember that clichés were such brilliantly evocative phrases when first coined that they entered the language and have stayed here ever since) the writer with style will always be seeking ways of conjuring up fresh pictures of the familiar.

But it's possible to go too far in striving for originality. As a young sports writer on a weekly newspaper I reported that the home football team's inside-forward was so very, very elusive that the visiting defenders found marking him was as difficult **as finding a needle in a cornfield**. 'No, lad,' said the veteran sports editor. 'Haystack, yes; but a cornfield is more than our readers can grasp!'

A further rebuke came during my time as a trainee feature writer on a national magazine which prided itself on the quality of its prose. Original copy had to be produced with extra-wide margins to accommodate the often scathing comments of first the Features Editor, then the Associate Editor and then the Editor – with each appending ever more critical afterthoughts on the copy's route back down to the apprehensive author.

Particularly dreaded were phrases which had been underlined and then ringed as 'cl' in the margin. House style was strictly No Clichés.

But on one occasion I was so incensed to see one of my most inventive phrases cl-ed that, forgetting my juniority, I burst into the office of the Associate Editor and blurted 'Mr Barker, I really must protest. In no way is this a cliché. While finishing this piece I stayed up till after midnight to polish that phrase. I can assure you it is totally original.'

The Associate Editor looked up from his desk, breathed heavily and said: 'Well, it reads like a cliché!'

Originality can be stretched too far.

8 The Joy of the Specialist

For many journalists the never-ending variety of their work is total fulfilment – some prefer to make one interest their very own

Writers who never aspire to a seat behind the executive desk dream of a career living their particular passion – as a motoring editor driving exotic cars at high speed across dramatic landscapes, as a fashion editor with a front row view of catwalk fantasies in jet-set locations, as a travel editor sampling the most glamorous destinations on earth, a food writer being bowed into the best restaurants, a film critic on chatting terms with the biggest names in Hollywood...

Indeed, a joyful way to earn a living.

But such specialists mentioned above may be called upon to serve many roles:

Motoring editor as Industrial Correspondent – explain why the Ford Motor Company is in trouble;

Fashion editor as Business Correspondent – will the merger of two fashion labels really work?

Travel editor as Political Correspondent – should holidaymakers be warned not to travel to a scene of terrorist threats?

Food writer as Consumer Watchdog – are supermarket own-brands good value?

Film critic as Social Commentator – can juvenile delinquency be blamed on excessive violence on screen?

The specialist becomes an MP to a whole constituency of responsibilities. If photogenic and articulate, he or she can become the public face of their industry.

Plying an ancient craft

For the greatest opportunity to revel in the written word the role of Travel Correspondent is hard to beat. It is an ancient craft.

Travellers' tales go back to when early man ventured from his cave and came back to tell what lay beyond the far horizon. The Greeks gave the process classic form, the Norsemen spun their epic sagas, medieval audiences could trace the footsteps of Chaucer and Marco Polo, Victorians thrilled to the accounts of Charles Dickens venturing into the Wild West of America and of explorers such as Richard Burton penetrating the furthest reaches of an empire on which they were assured the sun would never set – or, nearer home, could amble along with Robert Louis Stevenson on his *Travels with a Donkey*.

The twentieth century brought the extra dimension of photography, providing a window on the world so that armchair travellers could see what they were reading about. And now we live in an age when that window has been thrown wide open to exploit the immediacy of TV cameras carrying the viewer into the most remote corners of the planet.

Travel writing needs to match the immediacy of the TV camera, which takes the armchair traveller to the remotest parts of the earth

Seeing more than the view

Which gives the travel writer a very special need to produce Words That Make Pictures if they are to be read and not merely looked at.

Nick Trend, travel writer for the *Daily Telegraph*, warns about the temptation to produce general descriptions of beautiful settings rather than the telling details that give a real sense of place:

> The ramshackle sign on a beach tavern perhaps, or the way that the light catches the fragile branches of the tamarisk trees behind it. So, right from my very first trip, I have found that part of the excitement and challenge of the job is to try to mix a little verbal grit with that powdery sand; to add a fresh twist to those winding streets.
>
> But words can also do something that photographs struggle to do – they can tell a story; be it a historical anecdote or a moment of insight, or a remarkable encounter while travelling. That, for me, has become just as important as describing the view.

Brian Jackman, a distinguished travel correspondent of global perspective, adds a further dimension in his piece for the *Daily Telegraph* on whale-watching off the coast of Baja California:

> There is no wind and in the ensuing silence when the engines are switched off we can hear the breathing of the great whales all around us. First the hollow rush of expelled air from their great lungs, then the deep intake of air before the next dive.
>
> When they blow, sending columns of moisture 30ft into the air, the spray drifts over us, smelling faintly of cabbage, and when they surface to peer at us with curious, myopic eyes, it is impossible not to feel one's senses reaching out to them. Here we are – two species from alien planets – drawn together by mutual curiosity. And who, watching them come so trustingly close, can fail to be moved, knowing how we have persecuted these innocent beasts down the centuries?

S for Smell

The S in our formula of VISA covers Sounds as well as Speech and here we have sounds aplenty – the sounds of silence, heavy breathing and of columns of moisture being blown into the air. But Jackman adds a further S – that of Smell. And what a powerful element it is.

The description of a close encounter between two alien species is sensitively described but who will have ever read this feature without carrying for all time the knowledge that when great whales majestically blow they emit the smell of cabbage?

Jim Carrier also demonstrates the value of that extra S in visiting the Sherpas of the Himalayas for *National Geographic*:

> The full Khumbu moon lit the ice like frozen lightning as the shadows of the Sherpas slipped over my tent. I listen, half awake, to their gentle sounds: the jingle of the crampons, the creak of the backpacks, the resonant hum of the men chanting mantras. Juniper smoke, incense from their offering fire, seeped inside the tent, and I unzipped the flap to the pre-dawn chill. They gathered nearby to adjust their loads and drink hot milk tea. Then they were gone, winding through the jagged blocks of ice at the base of Mount Everest, trailed by a fading 'Ommmmmm'.

Again, the passage is full of evocative Sounds but what takes the reader right into that tent is the Smell of incense seeping inside from their offering fire.

'Smells are something not even 3D film in stereophonic sound can convey,' says Jackman, 'and yet they can capture the whole essence of a location.'

American travel writer Lee Marshall's first impression of Bangkok came from standing on a footbridge and watching the traffic by twilight:

> Below you, seven packed lanes of brake-lights flow sluggishly northwards, like corpuscles under a microscope, while the sweet smell of fossil fuel lingers in the air …

Here's another twilight view – Bill Bryson visiting Sorrento on his *Travels in Europe*:

> Lights began to twinkle on around the bay and were matched by the early-evening stars in the grainy blue sky. The air was warm and kind

Description of a romantic beauty spot takes an added dimension when the evening air carries the smell of fresh-baked bread

and had a smell of fresh-baked bread. This was as close to perfection as anything I had ever encountered.

This is how Rupert Everett, actor turned writer, describes the approach to Venice from the sea:

> As my water taxi enters the Grand Canal the scent of salt and diesel with its bottom note of sewage is delicious.

Adding that extra flavour

Rupert Everett's memoirs have been critically acclaimed as 'a triumph of observation and reverie' and include his description of Paris in August:

> Outside the streets were empty. The air was close, smelling of the sticky sap that oozed from the chestnuts and plane trees and stained the pavements around their roots. There was a wonderful silence during August in Paris, and the calls of wood pigeons, the distant murmur of traffic or the odd echo of a *mobilette* straining up some nearby cobbled street were all part of it.

No shortage of Sounds – pigeons, murmur of traffic, echo of a straining *mobilette*. But the Smell of the sticky sap beneath the trees is what lingers in the mind.

Jan Morris is a travel writer with a special interest in the human figures within the landscape – the people who inhabit the scenery. As in the back streets of Delhi from her book of *Destinations* (Oxford University Press):

> Through tortuous mucky lanes one approaches it from the busy highway, past the statutory Indian lines of beggars, crones and sadhus, through the spittle-stained portals where the old men stare, and into the intricate jumble of courts, tombs and arcades that surrounds the mosque of Nizamuddin and its sacred pool. Here mendicants lope around on knobbly staves, saintly scholars are at their books, sweet old ladies sit outside tombs (they are not allowed in, being female), and in the mosque there hustles and brushes the muezzin, an indefatigable goblin figure with white eyebrows and dainty tread. Nothing here is unpremeditated. All moves, although you might not guess it, to an immemorial schedule: the prayer call comes precisely to time, the rituals are meticulously ordered, even the whining beggars have their

In describing the landscape there is the chance to feature the people who inhabit the scenery appointed place in the hierarchy, and when I left the precincts the imam gave me his visiting card – his name is Al Haj Hazrat Peer Qazi Syed Sadfar Ali Nizami and his cable address is HEADPRIEST DELHI.

As Jan's eye records the bustling scene, her ear captures the sound of the call to prayer and the whining of the beggars. In observing the inflow of people from all parts of India, her nose provides another dimension:

> To the 'Sikhs and sleek Bengalis, Rajputs ablaze with jewellery, smart Gujaratis from the western coasts, beautiful Tamils from the south and black-veiled Moslem women' she adds: 'cloaked Tibetans smelling of untanned leather' and 'clerks from Bombay smelling of aftershave'.

First impressions

Brian Jackman explains that on stepping from a plane at a new destination he will pause to try and analyse the smell of what awaits him. So he would applaud Everett's description of arriving in Miami:

> As the doors of the plane open the wet scented Florida air rushes into the cabin. It smells of sun cream, air-conditioning and tropical drinks… Inside the terminal, the smell of damp carpet is the *eau de toilette* that will follow you around Florida. Rivers of delicious-smelling fitted carpet guide the traveller past gates to destinations that have only been dreamt about in the pages of Graham Greene and Ian Fleming…

Everett's acute sense of smell extends even to his description of fellow thespians:

- Orson Welles – 'looking like a mogul king … He was beautifully turned out in a grey suit and a shirt done up to the collar. No tie. He smelt vaguely of lemons';
- French actress Beatrice Dalle – 'a wild, unpredictable beauty tinged with the sparkle of madness. Her body was as full and ripe as a peach … and smelt deliciously of vanilla';
- Julia Roberts – 'like Madonna, smelt vaguely of sweat … after sex with a man she quite possibly fights the desire to eat him. For him, for all the hims, the smell of a superstar is a strange and powerful reminder, attractive and terrifying, of who is wearing the trousers. It marks him as her territory.'

For an acute observer even celebrities can be defined by their smell

Developing nasal powers

Few travel writers would claim to rival the extreme sensitivity of Everett's nasal passages but all would do well to develop whatever nasal powers they possess and give them full rein in seeking to achieve a truly total presentation of whatever they experience.

The motoring correspondent can capture the heady pungence of high-octane exhausts blasting from a pack of Grand Prix cars ... the fashion writer can seek to identify the wafting fragrances of the couture salon ... the film critic can always dismiss a would-be block-buster as a stinker ... and without the sharp nose of one travel writer how else would we ever learn that whales erupt with the smell of cabbage?

But however dramatic the A for Action, however colourful the V for Visuals or however vivid the S for Sounds (not forgetting Smells) the travel writer must also provide the fourth element of our VISA formula – I for Information.

However colourful and evocative, travel writing must also carry substance. The reader wants to learn hard facts about a destination as well as being presented with an attractive picture

Earth-shaking discovery

It can turn merely observing a distant scene into a reality that makes the reader actually want to go there. Writing for the *Daily Mail*, Paul Mansfield laid a captivating trail of facts to tempt visitors to head for the island of Martinique in the Caribbean:

> Fort-de-France, Martinique's capital, has an unmistakably French feel, with solid public buildings, cafés, corner boulangeries and parks with iron railings.
>
> In a hired car, I headed north, passing tiny villages where brightly coloured fishing boats were pulled up on the sand, and after an hour or so I reached the former capital of Saint Pierre.
>
> Back in the nineteenth century this was known as the Little Paris of the West Indies. Its waterfront was lined with warehouses and shops; there was an 800-seat theatre modelled on that of Bordeaux. Crinolined ladies and straw-boatered men strolled through the streets and horse-drawn trams clopped through the shady avenues.
>
> All of this came to an abrupt end on May 8, 1902, when Mont Pelee volcano, four miles away, blew its top with a force 40 times stronger than a nuclear bomb. The *Daily Mail*'s weekly edition of May 17 described the result; 'The whole city was buried in molten lava and was obliterated in three minutes. A total of 30,000 people died.'

Exploring the colonial past of a tourist attraction can provide rich material for the travel writer

> Today, Saint Pierre has a fascinating if spooky appeal.

So the reader already knows what to expect – what kind of atmosphere, what kind of architecture, what kind of cuisine, what will be the lingua franca. Even more, the promise of delivering a returning traveller's tale of a little-known tropical Pompeii.

Facts to tempt the traveller

Richard Robinson, of *The Times,* delivers a similarly arresting tailpiece in describing a Christmas break in Sanlucar de Barremeda on Spain's Atlantic coast:

> At the fringe of the town we stumbled into a vast flea market, gypsy linens billowing in the breeze, pigtailed Ecuadoreans selling bright Andean jumpers and clapping their arms against the chill. Beyond was a curious walled estate, overgrown with tussocky grass except for an impressive grove of giant palms. This was once the Botanic Garden, built long ago to acclimatise animals and plants brought from South America. The link between Sanlucar and the New World was strong, for it was here, intriguingly, that the Earth was proved to be round.

It was a discovery to change man's view of his planet. But who did the final calculation? How? When?

Robinson provides a bare fact that sets off the questions that will lead many of his readers to head for the place where the flat earth developed curves.

Travel writers go in the hope that others will follow.

9 The Disagreeable Art of the Columnist

Often hailed as the father of modern journalism, the first Lord Northcliffe proclaimed, 'News grabs, Features hold.' T'was ever thus

Newspapers pile on sales and the ratings of TV news channels soar when big stories break. But for most of the time the headlines have to feature the not-quite-so-extraordinary and the audience has to be tempted to return to the reassurance of the familiar.

In the case of TV, it is the faces of favourite newscasters and the styling of the studio furniture.

For newspapers, it is the band of feature writers who appear day after day, week after week, and give their journal its distinctive values.

Most prized of these are the big-name columnists, controversial masochists who ride the treadmill of churning out an endless flow of comment and opinion intended to surprise, stimulate and provoke. It is the most demanding of crafts; no sooner is one column finished then ideas for the next dominate the waking hours – ideas that will maintain a consistent personality and yet are essentially unpredictable.

Columnists do not do the obvious; the nearest they get is to expose the contradictions in the commonplace. Whenever possible they prefer disagreement to the consensus.

Big-money transfers

The biggest names may be compared to the stars of football's Premiership. They pull in the crowds, they establish loyal followings. So much so that they also feature in big-money transfers. To woo and win a rival's top columnist gives an editor the double prospect of adding that personal following to his own readership while diminishing the sales of the opposition.

Such a coup has sometimes led an editor to entice the newcomer with a salary greater than his own. And the expensive newcomer faces the challenge of inhabiting a very different environment.

Richard Littlejohn made his name as an outspoken columnist on the *Sun* newspaper in its years of supporting the Labour government. So he cheerfully sounded off thus in attacking the then leader of the Tory opposition:

Outspoken columnists will never retract their views – even if proved embarrassingly wrong

The sooner David Cameron gets a slap the better. I don't normally condone violence but I'm willing to make an exception for this upper-class podgy twerp.

Not content with telling us to hug a hoodie, the Eton eejit now wants us to love a lout. I don't want a Conservative leader to act as some second-rate social worker who puts the rights of the hoodlum before the rights of the victim …

Cameron has never and will never experience the struggle just to survive that most *Sun* readers have, and that's why he's not fit to be the leader of a scout group let alone the Opposition or, God forbid, the country.

Strong stuff. So how does Littlejohn retract when he is bought up by the ultra-Conservative *Daily Mail* and Cameron becomes Prime Minister? Does he shower him with praise? No way. That would be to admit he was wrong in the first case and big-name columnists don't do apologies. To prove he's consistent, Littlejohn merely turns his fire on Labour's leader of the Opposition and brands Ed Miliband 'a shameless opportunist' and 'a lunatic'. No U-turn there.

Bawdy partisanship

Possibly reflecting the bawdy partisanship of the House of Westminster, political columnists see their role as to challenge the consensus.

David Aaronovitch (contrarily an ex-communist who became a columnist for that one-time Voice of the Establishment, *The Times*) has declared that his views depart at least 90 degrees from the accepted view of things.

Mary Ann Sieghart, a fellow columnist on *The Times,* underwent a full 180-degree turn in the opening of a piece on the London mayoral election:

I used to think Ken Livingstone was a laugh. Many Londoners still do. But when I listen to his irresponsible comments, watch him break his promises with abandon and await with trepidation the extension of the congestion charge zone, it's not that I don't know whether to laugh or cry. I know exactly which to do.

The Mayor of London's behaviour isn't funny at all. It is dishonest, ill-judged and seemingly without conscience. He even prides himself on being shameless. When challenged by a London Assembly member for being 'slippery', he replied: 'I know, it's terrible, I get away with it all the time.' I wasn't there, but I imagine he had that Livingstonian smirk on his face.

    Why do we let him get away with it?

The columnist takes a magician's delight in projecting: 'Now you see it, now you don't' – leading the reader in one direction, then making a dramatic about-turn

Opening with an apparent contradiction is a favourite ploy of columnists. Having confessed that she used to find Livingstone amusing, Mary Ann Sieghart switches to not knowing whether to laugh or cry then promptly demonstrates why he reduces her to tears.

    Even the weightiest financial columnist will adopt a similar approach. Will Hutton of the *Observer* begins an assessment of the state of the nation by apparently celebrating the delights of being very, very rich:

> There has rarely been a better time to be a plutocrat. This is an unrivalled era in which both to acquire great wealth and keep it. Taxation on super-high incomes and vast fortunes is largely voluntary beyond a minimal contribution. Britain is at the foot of the international league tables for regulation. More extraordinarily still, criticism of extravagant wealth is culturally forbidden.

But after examining what he termed the City's 'Gadarene rush' to award its top executives excessive pay increases he concludes prophetically:

> Today's grossly unfair distribution of reward will one day create a backlash. Fairness is an elemental guiding human principle. The curious thing is that not one front-rank politician ventures a word of criticism. But this can't go on … can it?

Jeremy Warner, the *Daily Telegraph*'s economics columnist, sees his role as a 'mission to explain', adding 'and boy do economics, finance and business need a lot of explaining.'

> My aim is to demystify and make that world accessible. It is as much to shake readers out of their belief systems as to pander to them … Often, I'll end up being proved wrong, but if I can strike a chord, or stimulate debate in a well-informed and incisive manner, then it is mission accomplished.

One of the most prolific columnists (apart from writing best-selling books and devising a successful TV sitcom) is Caitlin Moran of *The*

Caitlin Moran has become a top columnist by following a policy of 'saying the unsayable'

Times who claims to say the unsayable on wildly random topics – Jam is horrible. Fish are evil. Ketchup shouldn't be kept in the fridge. Father Christmas is the sexiest man alive.

When it was suggested that serial killer Fred West was a victim of social deprivation by growing up in a family of eight living in grinding poverty, Caitlin (who describes herself as 'a working-class peasant') began her next column by declaring: 'My father raised eight children on welfare benefits and didn't kill any of us.'

(An opening to rival that of the *Daily Mirror*'s long-serving columnist, Cassandra [alias Bill Connor] who returned to his desk after six years' active service in World War Two and wrote: 'As I was saying when I was so rudely interrupted …')

Like most columnists, Caitlin delights in confounding her readers' expectations. She will announce: 'I've given up on high heels … The silver wedges, the green velvets, the black leather peep-toes with the bondage straps around the ankle. Even the canary-yellow ones that looked like they were from the 1930s, and made me feel like a chorus girl called Lola. All gone now.'

After listing the aching feet, the blisters, the dangers of tripping down steps and the cost of cab fares when walking even short distances is too painful, it is clear she is now going to settle down to a more staid form of footwear and possibly a quieter life.

But no. After several hundred more words luring the reader in that direction Caitlin finally reveals she is into 'flat green-and-gold brogues' so that at the end of a night out she can walk with the men to the pub, stay out to 3am – 'spending my cab money on champagne, and dancing'.

Confounding expectations

All is not frivolity, however.

The biggest response to any of her columns came when she wrote an imaginary letter to her teenage daughter to be read after her death, causing a world-wide explosion on social media when it was retweeted 23 million times.

Mercilessly lampooning celebrity postures, Caitlin will tackle areas of public concern – rape, wind turbines, closure of public libraries, lack of social care.

Despairing of the Establishment, she has published her own 14-point political manifesto (spelled 'Moranifesto'), including calls for proportional representation, the relocation of Parliament to

From the dangers of high heels on a night out to rape and social care – nothing is off the agenda

Birmingham, state-funding of political parties, legalisation of the sex industry and the restoration of the Victorian drinking fountain network – 'to save the 13 billion plastic water bottles thrown away every year'.

'The ultimate purpose of politics,' she insists, 'should be to enable people to experience as much joy as possible before they die. We are only here a tiny wink of time – a snap of the fingers; barely enough time to get a proper round in.'

There's that final throwaway – a reminder that these are the views of a working-class peasant who quite likes a drink or two. Columnists must never be pompous.

All too familiar onslaught

Attacking pop star Liam Gallagher's opinion of the rehab troubles of a couple of middle-class rockers ('Posh boys can't take drugs, man, they're lightweights') the *Observer Magazine*'s Barbara Ellen described his remarks as 'irresponsible, inflammatory and "classist"'.

The reader prepares for an all too familiar onslaught on the likes of Gallagher but Barbara confounds all expectations by adding: 'and almost certainly true'. She elaborates:

> An adolescence spent reading your poetry out loud to mummy in the school hols (jolly good feedback), drinking cans of pop too fast and then going for a skip through the spring flowers is not the greatest apprenticeship for an existence at the stinky knife edge of rock'n'roll … Letting these sorts of people anywhere near drugs is like letting kittens play with dynamite.
>
>   Whatever happens (is Barbara's conclusion) the Posh Boys should keep the rehab sob stories to a minimum. In the crazy world of sex, drugs and rock'n'roll there's no need to make quite such a song and dance about it.

Letting fly at any target

So long as their values remain consistent, columnists can let fly at any target – from the City to the Royal Family, from the Health Service to Ryanair, from footballers' wives to social workers, from energy prices to shortages of plumbers.

However varied their targets, columnists must display a consistent set of values

Here the *Guardian*'s resident humorist, Charlie Brooker, exposes a danger of social media:

Many women columnists seek to provoke by displaying unexpected insight into everyday domestic life

Not so long ago, if you wanted to issue a 13-year-old girl with a blood-curdling death threat, you had to scrawl it on a piece of paper, wrap it round a brick, hurl it through her bedroom window, and scarper before her dad ran out of the front door to beat you insensible with a dustbuster. Now, thanks to Twitter, hundreds and thousands of people can simultaneously surround her online, screaming abuse until she bursts into tears. Hooray for civilisation.

Describing Twitter as 'a hothouse in which viral outbreaks of witless bullying can be incubated and unleashed before anybody knows what's happening', he issues this final advice:

Bitch all you like. Just don't be a dick about it. Poise, people. Poise.

More restrained language is favoured by the many women columnists who seek to shed light on the trials of family life – from the bitchiness of other mums at the school gate to coping with in-laws, from crash diets to the loss of the local post office. Rather than striking out, they seek to strike a chord with their fellow women.

Who would not identify with the opening sentence of Angela Epstein's column in *You Magazine* of November 5, 2006?

Victoria Beckham and I have never had that much in common.

The piece continues:

A penchant for size 4 jeans, perhaps – though my interest in them faded once I'd left primary school and they no longer fitted me. But I really do understand Posh's current preoccupation. Rumour has it that, with three sons under her tiny belt, the ex-Spice Girl is desperate to have a daughter. Three years ago I was in exactly the same situation.

Already proud mother to a trio of schoolboys, I suddenly became wildly broody. Did I want another baby or did I simply want a baby because I wanted a little girl. Well, I wanted the first but I was going crazy for the second.

Going on the describe both the trials and delights of succeeding in her ambition ('Each morning my daughter and I are locked in a battle of wills as she rejects the clothes I want her to wear, slinging them on the floor like a professional Topshop customer'), Angela concludes:

I adore my little girl. But she is a shameless diva, ruthless despot and practised manipulator. One day, in years to come, as we stroll arm-linked, through a cosy and companionable mother–daughter moment, I'll remind her of that. Just as my mother did me.

Putting a sting in the tail

That last sentence constitutes a columnist's most powerful weapon – the sting in the tail. Having had her fellow mothers nodding along with her vivid descriptions of the demands of the evolving female of the species, she delivers a jolt by confessing that she gave her mother the same problems. And leaves her readers having to ask themselves: 'I suppose I did, too.'

Another example of leading the reader up the wrong path comes from Carol Midgley of *The Times*. Addressing the suggestion that school uniforms are for squares and losers, she writes:

> I detested school uniform. As a lumpen, self-conscious 13-year-old, having to pull on a fizzing mass of shapeless viscose (which made me resemble a sea cow in a navy tunic) felt like being the daily butt of a local-authority joke. Thanks for that. Obviously, girls then as now pulled the usual tricks to 'sophisticate' the sea-cow look: hitching up A-line skirts to parade corned-beef thighs chapped by Lancashire winds, stuffing socks down bras and tying shirts in a knot to reveal dough-white stomachs Biroed with 'Daryll 4 Me'. If the aim of a uniform was to instil discipline, then, at our comp at least it was an epic fail.

How many women would not agree with that? So Carole was obviously going to urge that school uniforms should be scrapped. She continues:

> God, no. Are you mad? The alternative is far worse, as I discovered at sixth form college where I could wear what I liked. Suddenly, getting dressed each day became excruciating; imagining the amused, gimlet eyes of the popular well-dressed, cool, wealthier girls scanning your one pair of cheap, high-waisted stonewashed jeans.

Arguing that no one can remain seriously vain in a school uniform, Carole sums up:

Successful columnists need to be able to deliver that all-important pay-off line

Humans have the rest of their lives to be judged on and obsessed by their clothes. At least let the school years be a respite from that. Rich or poor, pretty or plain, school uniforms truly are one of life's great levellers. They manage to make everyone look crap.

Would-be columnists should note the total self-confidence and unrelenting stamina needed for the job, the use of colourful analogy, the ability to render a major topic trivial and to elevate the trivial to the talking point of the day for their devoted followers.

And as columnists take increasingly to the social media pages on the world-wide web, that talking point can easily become a point of gossip around the globe.

10 Digging for Anecdotes

In applying the rule of 'If you state it, prove it' the need to provide the relevant anecdote is vital and will become memorable for the reader

The staple content of after-dinner speakers and visiting celebrities on TV chat shows, anecdotes are thus widely seen as the telling of amusing incidents. But anecdotes can be sad as well as funny, emotional as well as flippant, dramatic as well as gentle. They are the strongest element in the A for Action of our Hallmarking system.

What they have in common is that they describe a happening and – whether brief or longer – that they tell a story with a beginning, a middle and an end. Their value is that people can remember stories more easily than mere statements and as smaller stories distributed throughout the big story they provide a welcome change of pace – as demonstrated by our Hallmark-coding exercise in analysing the structure of successful features

In an earlier chapter, anecdotes were described as 'golden nuggets' but they are not strewn carelessly in the writer's path; they so often require hard digging to extract their full value.

The trouble is that most people do not think in anecdotes; their memories become blurred by time, the past a generalized well-trodden path leading to whole episodes being dismissed in a single phrase.

So how to wrest anecdotes from a blank-minded subject?

Imagining what might have happened

This is where the journalist has to think like a playwright or novelist. Had he created such an imaginary character for a work of fiction what might have befallen him or her to grab the interest of the reader? And whatever ideas you bring to the surface are then used to prod the subject's memory.

At the mundane level of marking the retirement of the town's oldest taxi driver for the local paper, these questions may well spark some colourful material:

> Have you ever been asked to follow that cab? What's the longest fare you have ever had? Where to and why? Biggest tip? Who gave it? Most famous passenger? Strangest passenger? Ever threatened by a passenger? Ever come across a roadside emergency?

Suggestions of happenings most likely to have taken place will often prod the memory sufficiently to produce anecdotes of very different incidents that really did occur

Such questions might summon up cliché situations but very often they will provoke totally unexpected answers.

As a young reporter, I was sent to interview a rural midwife who had been appointed OBE after 50 years of selfless service. Wearing her best pinafore, she received me in the 'front room' of her tiny cottage and invited me to join her in a glass of sweet sherry to mark her award. She was pleasant and desperately trying to be helpful but the interview proved difficult.

'How many births have you delivered?'

'No idea. Must have been hundreds.'

'What was the most unusual birth?'

'They're all pretty much the same after a time.'

'Any triplets, quads, sextuplets?'

'No, that sort of thing tends to happen in hospitals.'

'What was the longest labour?'

'When you're on the job you have no idea of time.'

So much for the obvious. The interview was getting nowhere. So I tried a different approach:

'As a country midwife, have you ever delivered a baby in the open air?'

'Good Lord, no. Whatever made you think of such a thing?'

Then she screwed up her eyes in thought, pursed her lips and after a long pause added: 'Well, there was the time I was called out in the middle of the night to the gipsy encampment on the heath and there was this young gipsy girl writhing in agony inside a sort of bivouac flapping in the wind. She was in need of a breech delivery and her parents were just looking on helplessly, not knowing what to do. I got her transferred to one of the caravans and managed to sort out the problem. If they hadn't thought to send for me the mother and baby would both have been goners.'

A race against time

Thus encouraged, I tried a different line:

'Have you ever been involved in a race against time – perhaps like a home-birth mother developing dangerous complications and needing to be rushed to the hospital for emergency treatment?'

'No, nothing like that. I reckon I could deal with most complications.' Then, again the frown of concentration and a sudden jog of memory: 'Well, it wasn't me in the rush to the hospital but the husband of one of my patients panicked when the wife went into very premature contractions and instead of calling me he stuck her in the back of the car and drove at full tilt towards the hospital.

'However, I was called out – but by the police. The car had crashed en route and the mother-to-be was trapped inside. When I got there the car was a right mess. They couldn't open the doors because the bodywork was all twisted and so the poor woman couldn't be got out. She was still conscious and I could see the birth was well on the way. So I got a policeman to smash the rear window so I could crawl inside and deliver the baby on the back seat.'

Questions that provoke unexpected answers

Neither of my questions produced anything like the answers I might have expected. Instead they gave me two powerful anecdotes that lifted my story to the top of the page in the next week's paper.

In each case I chose to describe the events largely in the third person to build up a sense of drama that her simple quotes could not convey.

Digging for a humble anecdote can sometimes unearth a major story.   And stories don't come much humbler than the local paper's standby – stories of 'people with interesting jobs'.

One such was about a man, armed with a brush and paste-pot, who was regularly seen atop a 20ft extending ladder, assembling the jigaw that was the various sections of a giant poster on a billboard overlooking the town's principal shopping centre. In days long pre-dating health-and-safety concerns, the foot of the ladder merely rested on the pavement; there was no workmate to stand watch.

He stolidly insisted that he'd never fallen off, never had a high wind blow the ladder to a precarious angle, never had a passing vehicle nudge the bottom of the ladder, never completed pasting together the most complicated of posters only to come down to ground and look up to see that he hadn't put it together in the right sequence – perhaps the main advertising slogan reading from back to front? No, nothing like that. It was just another job and he quite enjoyed looking down on the rest of the population.

Final question (in desperation): But surely there must have been some hairy moments working at that height?

Came the astonishing reply: 'You don't scare easily when you've been A-bombed and lived to tell the tale.'

Yes, this modest bill-poster was part of a team of Allied POWs doing forced labour on the dockside at Nagasaki when the Americans

In attempts to unearth anecdotes the writer must lead the way. Most people are unlikely to offer up memorable moments in their life

Searching for a simple anecdote on a weekly paper can open up a major story worthy of national coverage

dropped the world's second atomic weapon on the Japanese port in August, 1945. The nuclear blast hurled him into the water and a reverse tsunami carried him far out to sea where he was rescued by a fishing boat.

Instantly, the story about a man with an interesting job gave way to a lead feature on the town's most remarkable inhabitant. This in turn became a national talking point when it emerged he was struggling to secure a war pension in face of the military authorities' previous denials that any Allied personnel were in Nagasaki when it was chosen as an atomic target.

Some anecdote.

Snakes and a ladder

Similarly, a bank security guard proved a difficult subject. Not a single anecdote emerged from a whole range of questions. No, he had never thwarted a bank raid. No, he had never been ambushed while riding shotgun on a transfer of cash. No. he had never caught out a counter clerk embezzling funds.

'It might sound a very exciting job but it's mainly boring routine,' he said and then this Cockney-born unassuming individual added: 'I can't wait for when my shifts allow me to spend a quiet weekend in the New Forest and earn a bit of pocket money.'

How?

'By catching a few snakes.'

What?

'Yes, you see in my spare time I'm a professional snake-catcher.'

He explained how he would take a train to Brokenhurst, go to a nearby builder's yard, borrow a few sheets of corrugated iron, wander round the forest and place them on the ground in various sites, book into a favourite pub and spend Friday and Saturday eating, drinking and playing darts with the locals, then at midday on Sunday he would go back to where he had left the corrugated iron sheets and, wearing thick gloves, he would pick them up..

And there, lying in neat rows, would be a collection of poisonous adders, attracted by the heat generated by sunshine on the metal grooves which also, as a series of miniature tunnels, provided protection from overhead attack.

Back in London on Monday morning, he would sell the snakes to a laboratory on the Great West Road which needed live venom to produce the necessary serum to treat victims of snake-bite.

Suddenly, here was a much more interesting story than the everyday life of a bank guard; here was a man with a most unusual hobby.

So what started it off?

'Well, I done a bit before when I was appointed snake-catcher for the 14th Army in Burma during the war.'

What?

'A lot of the troops fresh out from England were so scared of snakes when sent into the jungle they would panic and run if any kind of snake slithered into view – sometimes meaning a carefully planned ambush of Japanese troops would have to be abandoned. So they had to be given the confidence of being issued with life-saving serum.

'And that meant someone had to be parachuted into snake-infested territory occupied by the enemy, catch some of the most dangerous snakes in that area, then smuggle them back through the enemy lines so they could be dispatched to a serum-producing establishment in India which then sent the necessary supplies to our advancing troops before they ventured into that stretch of jungle.

'That someone was me. After a quick course in snake-handling I almost enjoyed it. After all, my job was to dodge the enemy and that seemed a lot safer than trying to kill them.'

An incredible reward for a journalist bothering to question why a bank guard chose to spend quiet weekends in the New Forest.

Importance of the throwaway line

Making the most of an anecdote calls upon the storyteller's craft – establishing the setting and atmosphere, creating a sense of uncertainty, then delivering a punchline denouement.

An example is the throwaway line of a Welsh paramedic recalling one of the most tragic accidents he had attended – in which an elderly couple returning home from a celebratory dinner were crushed to death when the roof of a road tunnel collapsed on their car just as they were about the clear the exit.

'Just think,' the paramedic told a local reporter, 'a minute or so later getting there and the tunnel would have already collapsed and they could have turned back and gone another way. A matter of seconds earlier and the roof would have fallen down behind them.'

A strong anecdote as it is, but the incident could have been much strengthened by some elementary digging and imaginative storytelling.

Enquiries at the hotel and of friends would have enabled a description of a widow and widower enjoying a candlelit dinner to

However attractive an anecdote, it can be rewarding to pose an extra question: 'And what happened next?'

mark the anniversary of their meeting by way of a dating agency. 'Coffee?' asks the waiter as the meal nears its end. 'No thanks,' says the woman, reaching across the table to take the hand of her partner. 'I think we'll have an early night.'

Half an hour later their car is driving through the tunnel, only three more miles to home. Then the tunnel roof caves in on them. It took several days to recover their bodies from beneath hundreds of tons of rubble.

'What a pity,' says the hotel waiter when he learns of the tragedy, 'that I didn't persuade them to stay for coffee.'

Such is the power of an anecdote to transform a traffic statistic into a poignant human drama.

11 Pencil or Recorder?

Modern technology is transforming journalism in many ways but there is still one area where an old-fashioned skill cannot be denied

Second only to their initial complaint about the 'kindergarten' use of highlighters to colour-code features, the freshers at Bournemouth University were quick to protest at the news that at the end of a three-year course in multimedia journalism – embracing print, radio, video and the web – they would be required to have attained a speed of 100 words a minute in shorthand.

'How old-fashioned!' was a typical reaction. 'Who needs a pencil and notebook when most mobile phones enable you to make an audio recording?'

Yet three years later, they came to see that mention of a shorthand speed on their CVs was often the factor that caught an editor's eye and at least gained them a job interview. This was not a case of nostalgic regard for the days of 'real journalists'. For all the digital wizardry available to the twenty-first century journalist, the pencil is still their most valuable tool.

A TV journalist confesses

One of my visiting lecturers, a famous TV journalist, confessed his regret at never having learned shorthand:

'There's always that vital throwaway quote in an unlikely spot at an unexpected moment. Or the call with a last-minute revelation from a key contact just before you go on air. No time to set up a recording and yet a worrying factor in having to rely on memory when taken by surprise or in a rush.'

Recorders are not allowed in courtrooms, useless at the back of a crowded press conference and a stultifying instrument when dashing around to secure instant quotes from incoherent eye-witnesses of some disaster.

Recorders, however sophisticated, are still machines and machines go wrong – often at the most unreasonable times. And total reliance on recorders can lead to the disengagement of memory so that the sudden blankness of the machine is matched by an embarrassing blankness of the brain. The interview is lost in space.

True to the guiding principles of Words That Make Pictures there follow a couple of anecdotes to illuminate such a dilemma.

When it comes to interviewing, technology can be a doubtful friend

In my early days as a magazine writer, even so-called portable tape recorders were pretty cumbersome. It was a thrill therefore to be the first man in the office sent on assignment with a new-fangled, pocket-sized wire-recorder, replacing quarter-inch tape with wire as thin as cotton thread and still claiming to deliver satisfactory reproduction.

The mission was to gather material for me to 'ghost' (see following chapter) a feature in the name of Matt Busby, already legendary as the manager of Manchester United, on why his team looked set to achieve football's coveted Double – winning the League Championship and the FA Cup in the same season.

Matt Busby turned out to be a genial, uncle-like figure with a warm Scottish accent. We met in his office at Old Trafford with the wire-recorder placed on the desk between us as I started the interview. He provided intriguing insight into the psychology of football, describing his methods for assessing the mental strength of individual players and the ploys he used to achieve maximum motivation.

I listened, fascinated, as he explained why the Double was so difficult, why the best team in the country at winning League matches week after week could be surprisingly toppled by lesser opposition in the Cup.

'Why would a sprinter who records a 10-second sprint on a stadium track fail to manage anything like that time if you asked him to run along a cliff-top path, with a sheer fall into the sea immediately on his right? In the stadium he concentrates on running. On the cliff-top he has one eye on the edge. That's how it is when you are playing in a knock-out competition – the main emotion is a fear of falling.'

An undignified exit

Great stuff! I was effusive with my thanks as I ended the interview, picked up the wire-recorder and went to leave the room. The problem was that everything on the desk top started to leave with me. I realized with horror that the wire had come off its spool and – virtually invisible – had twisted itself into knots around the telephone, a silver-framed portrait of the Busby family, a plastic in-tray and a mahogany tobacco stand for the manager's favourite pipe.

The more I tugged, the greater the jumble of objects the wire entangled. Appreciating my confusion, Matt Busby summoned his secretary to bring in a pair of scissors and cut free the tangled mess. I could only watch as my brilliant interview was literally reduced to shreds. And I was so much in awe of this new technology I had not bothered to take the elementary precaution of taking a note!

It was the birth of an undying devotion for the United manager when he gave me a broad smile and said: 'If you've got a pencil and notebook, perhaps we should start again.'

Which we did – and he liked the resurrection of my 'ghosted' feature so much he sent me two tickets for that season's Cup Final at Wembley (where Manchester United narrowly failed to win the Double).

A moment of horror

Veteran interviewer Lynn Barber did not have such an understanding subject when experiencing the worst-ever 'horror' of a tape recorder breakdown while conducting a session with Sir David Attenborough.

In her memoirs, she writes:

> 'I saw the light flickering and realised my batteries were fading but he was not sympathetic. Consequently, while everyone else reveres him as a national treasure, I can only remember the cold glint in his eye, the drumming fingers, while I fiddled cack-handedly with my batteries.'

Lynn now works with two recorders.

My near-disaster at Old Trafford perhaps explains the speedy demise of the wire-recorder and although I made great use of subsequent generations of more efficient devices it was never without a pencil and notebook to hand.

It is important to appreciate that people react differently when confronted with a recorder. Some subjects, often public figures, can be wary, stilted – fearful that a careless indiscretion might come back to haunt them if subsequently broadcast to the world.

Conductor wielding a pencil

Others revel in the thought that their pearls of wisdom are being captured for posterity and will happily prattle on without drawing breath. This is where the writer has to exert control over the machine, to remind himself that he is conducting the interview and that the pencil is his baton.

Picking it up to make a shorthand note only when the interviewee

Why a famous interviewer makes a point of always employing **two** recorders releases relevant information is an effective signal that you would like more of the same. Pointedly putting it down when the subject wanders off track is a polite way of stemming the flow.

'Yes, that was very interesting but could we go back to your time in Africa …?'

The advantage of this method is that you are editing the interview as you go along. By jotting down only the significant quotes you are already assembling the core of the story; by merely listening during the interview you face the task of returning to the office and having to wade through a mass of irrelevant chatter to pick out the salient points. In effect, you are conducting the interview twice over – this time interviewing the machine.

A journalist wearing L-plates

The process of mastering shorthand is like learning to drive a car. For a would-be motorist still displaying L-plates, the requirements of changing gear, making handbrake starts, reversing into a parking bay and remembering to look into the rear mirror as well as straight ahead are all deliberate, self-conscious actions. Once past the Test, they gradually flow into your subconscious and you can concentrate on simply driving.

The laborious early stages of learning shorthand consist of dismantling the English language into a series of squiggles and dots that go above, through and below the line and then seeking to put them together as quickly as possible so that they represent words again. Speed comes with relentless practice and shorthand is only effective when your pencil can transform speech into meaningful outlines without the brain being engaged.

Once that becomes an automated process, you enjoy the advantage of being able to concentrate on observing body language and simultaneously on listening to and evaluating what is being said.

If the salesman's gift of the gab enables a journalist to win the confidences of complete strangers, the ability to be a good listener is paramount.

Only when you listen can you tell it like it is.

12 Who Wants to Be a Ghost?

Whether or not a writer welcomes the chance to 'ghost' a story is largely a matter of ego – no one will know I wrote it; why should the credit go to someone who can't write it himself?

Andrew Crofts, one of Britain's most successful ghostwriters, positively revels in being the invisible man granted access to the inner lives of those whose vanity demands their name on the cover of a book and yet need a professional hand to deliver the words they cannot summon for themselves.

'Behind the title of ghostwriter, I could converse with kings and billionaires as easily as whores and actors,' Crofts declares. 'I could stick my nose into everybody else's business and ask all the impertinent questions I wanted to to. At the same time I could also live the pleasant life of a writer ...'

Learning that Crofts averages six-figure fees for passing off celebrity memoirs, some writers go so far as to dismiss ghosting as a form of prostitution. Yet it can be a most satisfying art. As a playwright gives the characters he creates a distinctive vocabulary and manner of delivery so the ghostwriter has to capture the individual speech patterns of the person that his words seek to imitate. All too often, a journalist wants to write the story in his own way and then merely append the name of the subject.

Life stories that fail to convince

Which explains why so many celebrity 'autobiographies' fail to convince:

- When an England wicket-keeper sprinkles his alleged memoirs with quotes from Rudyard Kipling and Robert Louis Stevenson and discusses the 'choking and claustrophobic Bradford that J. B. Priestley wrote about so nostalgically in *English Journey* during the mid-1930s'. Hardly the authentic voice of a Yorkshire lad who dropped out of schooling at 19 to become a professional cricketer and litters his conversation with 'blooming heck'.
- When a star footballer, whose post-match interviews on screen reveal a lack of basic education, fluently discusses in print the advantages of the 'holding pattern of the midfield echelon'.
- When the memoirs of a long-battered pugilist claim that he 'found spiritual solace in the moment of defeat'.
- When a TV comedian with a reputation for coarse humour produces

Dialogue given to a character must always match his true identity

a flow of effortless prose to describe 'the magical chemistry of playing to live audiences'.

John Wilcox, a former journalist who became a successful writer of fictional military history, was named Provincial Young Journalist of the Year in his early days as a reporter.

One of the stories which made his name concerned the driver of a Number 26 bus in Birmingham who finished his shift, parked his bus in the depot, said goodnight to his mates and walked out into the night – never to reappear. At least, not for seven years. Then, one morning he walked into the depot, wearing his old uniform, and went to climb into the cab of the Number 26 bus as usual. Noting the consternation around him, he smiled and declared: 'In the words of Mark Twain, reports of my death have been greatly exaggerated.'

Half a century later, Wilcox admits to an abiding embarrassment at ever attributing such a quote to a Birmingham bus driver. 'It's most unlikely he was conversant with the works of Mark Twain and so would have offered a much more basic reason for his long absence. I chose to be clever and in doing so destroyed the credibility of the story.'

Wilcox was not ghosting as such but the lesson holds good for whatever words writers put into the mouths of characters they want their readers to believe in. Would they have really said it like that? Would they have written it like that?

Unseen workers beneath Walt Disney World

Robert Harris's best-selling novel, *The Ghost* (Arrow Books, 2008), tells of a writer hired to produce the memoirs of a controversial former prime minister. The central character defines the craft of the ghostwriter: 'We are the phantom operatives who keep publishing going, like the unseen workers beneath Walt Disney World. We scuttle along the subterranean tunnels of celebrity, popping up here and there, dressed as this character or that, preserving the seamless illusion of the Magic Kingdom.'

Being invited to ghost a political autobiography is in contrast to the hero's more likely chores such as 'the memoirs of a TV magician who had – of course – been abused in childhood but who had used his skill as an illusionist to conjure up a new lifestyle etc etc'.

Robert Harris, a former TV reporter, newspaper columnist and

Ghosts writers are 'phantom operatives … unseen workers … scuttling along the subterranean tunnels of celebrity – expecting no glory.'

political editor, sought the advice of experienced ghostwriters before beginning the novel and it becomes something of a minor handbook for would-be practitioners in that every chapter is prefaced by a tip from Andrew Croft's book, *Ghostwriting* (A & C Black, 2004).

Declaring 'a ghost must expect no glory', Crofts likens the role to that of a psychiatrist sitting by the patient on a couch – listening to self-justifications, understanding motivation, prodding unwelcome memories.

'I have often been told by subjects,' writes Crofts, 'that by the end of the research process they feel as if they have been in therapy.' He also states: 'Quite often, particularly if you are helping them write a memoir or autobiography, the author will dissolve into tears when they're telling the story … Your job under these circumstances is to pass the tissues, keep quiet and keep recording.'

Get up from the couch

But the job of the ghostwriter is more than listening to someone speaking into a recorder. If an autobiography is a profile writ large, then all those eight elements on the 'dartboard' in the earlier chapter have to be explored at much, much greater depth. It is most unlikely that the subject can supply all that from memory so you have to get up from that couch, switch off the recorder and go in search of the required material.

And again the VISA formula applies:

Visuals – readers wants to see the world through his eyes and share his thoughts. They want to see him as a boy and the backstreet into which he was born, to see him lost in an African landscape, to see him with the women in his life, to see him facing a crowd of hecklers. They want to share his thoughts on a rise from poverty to riches, on the loss of a best friend, on taking his place in Parliament, on unfulfilled dreams …

Information – the need for detailed research. The subject was expelled from school so obtain a copy of his last report. Who were the witnesses on the day of that fateful third wedding? Which travel company provided the disastrous itinerary for that African safari? What was the state of the stock market when his company went bust? When exactly was he first chosen to contest the by-election which launched him into politics? How did *The Times* record his major triumph?

Sounds – a memoir is in effect one long quote so readers are mentally

The journalist as psychiatrist can provide effective therapy

Lack of familiarity can be an advantage. The ghost will be asking the same obvious questions as the reader, making a specialist subject open to a wider audience

listening to the subject's voice throughout. Which is why the voice must ring true. And it's a tone the ghost must maintain over the length of a whole book.

Action – the key ingredient is the anecdote. If it has been defined as a happening, that makes a lifetime one long series of happenings and, as we have established, the majority of people tend not to think in neatly assembled anecdotes. So you will have to visit the scene of key incidents, interview other participants, establish the context of what took place.

Although personally enthusiastic about the business of ghosting, Crofts warns that it is not an easy way to make a living.

But there are two advantages:

- No agonising over structure – a memoir provides the guarantee of a satisfying beginning, a middle and an end.
- The less you know about the subject's profession the more copies of the book are likely to be sold.

Never hesitate to ask stupid questions

By not being afraid to ask the elementary question and getting an answer, the ordinary reader will understand you are opening up to a much wider audience.

Although not familiar with motor racing, I was once asked to ghost Stirling Moss's account of surviving a near-fatal crash at the Spa circuit in Belgium. I sat at the injured racing driver's bedside in St Thomas's Hospital, London, as he talked me through a set of pictures which showed a rear wheel breaking off and overtaking the car.

'It was a practice day and I took my Lotus out on the circuit to scrub the tyres,' he was saying.

'What kind of brush do you use for that?' I asked.

Moss nearly fell out of the bed, laughing.

'We used to scrub new tyres by sliding the car from side to side to make them slicker,' he explained (this being in the days when it was left to the drivers to seek greater speed by making their tyres as smooth as possible).

I ghosted Moss on many subsequent occasions and, while he never ceased to poke fun at me for such ignorance, he acknowledged that if a writer doesn't understand, neither will the reader. From then on, I never hesitated to ask the stupid question.

Although memoirs and autobiographies are of the non-fiction category, publishers often prefer novelists as ghostwriters. Many choose to accept the generous cheques anonymously but it is becoming an increasingly respectable practice and Booker Prize winner Paddy Doyle broke cover to proclaim that he ghosted the controversial memoirs of footballer Roy Keane, *The Second Half* (Weidenfeld and Nicolson, 2014). Not only are novelists accustomed to evoking scenes and emotions, they have the stamina to produce words by the many, many thousands. Feature-writing journalists, by contrast, are at most middle-distance runners, usually required to produce from 1,000 to 3,000 words at the most. Taking on a book is a marathon task.

This was brought home to me when I approached a publisher with a proposal to ghost the memoirs of a socialite beauty newly released from prison after a notorious career as an international drugs smuggler, operating a fleet of ex-World War Two motor torpedo boats out of Tangier.

I met her when she was living off her ill-gotten gains in a hotel in Majorca and the publisher insisted that she came to London to discuss a possible contract. The editorial director who took us for lunch in a Soho restaurant was a distinctly staid character with the appearance and manner of a Victorian solicitor. But he quickly melted in the presence of this beautiful woman who was consciously making him the target of her considerable charms, regaling him with accounts of her wild escapades and many love affairs.

As coffee neared, he took a deep breath and the Victorian solicitor reappeared to say: 'We have looked at Peter's synopsis and there is obviously a very colourful story to be told. But before we go ahead I have to warn you that although many people think they have a book in their lifetime experience it might prove to be a life that runs to only 10,000 words or even 20,000 words.

'To make a book we're looking for no less than 80,000 to 100,000 words. Before we go any further, are you satisfied you can provide us with that much material?'

My companion leaned over the table, planted her lipstick on his bashful cheek and said: 'Don't worry, darling. If I find we're running short, I'll go out and live a few more chapters.'

Such are the delights of becoming a ghost.

If journalists can be regarded as at the most middle-distance runners, they face a marathon when writing a book

CHARITY CYCLIST'S TRAGIC DEATH

Banned from the major television channels for several years after a series of drinks-drugs-sex scandals, Dave Delaney, the former child star-turned disc jockey had accepted the challenge to cycle from John O'Groats to Lands End to raise funds for a children's charity. The idea was to prove he was now 'clean' in mind and body, a man of compassion.

But he was already two days behind schedule on his 1,000-mile mission and the previous evening his business manager had phoned to say his sponsors were beginning to worry that he would not meet the plan for his arrival at a children's hospital near Lands End to be screened live on a peak-time TV programme.

When his support riders had stopped that morning to take on water from a roadside fountain, Delaney had slipped into the village pub, grabbed a bottle of Coke and a Brandy and drank from both, complaining his 'guts felt queer'. A couple of hours later, he was seen furtively swallowing a handful of white pills – 'my little white clouds,' he cheerfully explained.

Nearing the top of a steep ascent on a bleak Lancashire moor, his bike suddenly went into a zig-zag, pitching him on to a rocky bank. When Dave Delaney's limp body was pulled from his bike, his fingers had to be pealed from the handlebars one by one – the death-grip agony of massive cardiac failure in his desperate effort to revive a once glittering career.

The first to reach him found his face turning yellow, his eyes bulging. Mouth to mouth and chest massage produced nothing but a drawn-out bubbling from his lungs, the smell of brandy still on his breath.

A local doctor rushing to the scene pronounced him dead. Pulling up the rider's jersey to examine the body, two more tubes of white amphetamine pills were revealed. Shaking his head, the doctor murmured: 'Drink and drugs; a crazy mix.'

But David Delaney was well aware of the risk hidden in his little white clouds. He had no choice but to die in the attempt to resurrect a career long dead.

The last words on that remote hillside from a voice which once commanded audiences of millions had been: 'Its all right. Get me back on my bike. I want to go on ...'

13 The Writer as Sub-Editor

If writers and photographers traditionally observe a wary relationship, regarding themselves as of separate species, writers have constantly feuded with sub-editors

As a breed, writers tend to regard themselves as the free spirits of journalism – roving far and wide to produce the creative spark of their publications only to have their precious copy savaged by insensitive desk-bound souls.

In turn, the sub-editors see most writers as feckless egoists who show no appreciation of the subbing process which turns their dross into golden prose.

In fact, the sub-editor is the key figure in the whole editorial process, establishing the quality control of the content and producing the compulsive headings, standfirsts, captions and display quotes which pull the readers into the pages. They see themselves as the conscience of the publication and writers can only benefit if they come to appreciate that role.

A first step to that is to take a deep breath and regard their own finished copy with the detached eye of a sub-editor.

- Is it of the commissioned length?
- Is it written to the style of the target publication?
- Have the facts been at least double-checked?
- Are there any grammatical and punctuation lapses?
- Are there any spelling mistakes that the laptop's spell-check couldn't read?
- Is punctuation consistent?
- And, overall, is the piece structured most effectively?
- Does the heading grab attention?
- Is there an intriguing intro?
- Does the ending encompass the whole story?

Self-criticism to this extent does not come easy to many writers who have laboured on the research and agonized over composition. For them, the material is all too obvious, the context firmly mixed in their minds, the shape seen as a thing of beauty.

But only by being prepared to take an objective view of their own work can writers (increasingly required to be their own sub-editor) expect to have their copy sufficiently polished to transfer to the printed page without undue interference.

Turn overleaf and see how 13 elements of the piece of 'raw' copy opposite needed the sub-editor's attention.

THE SUB-EDITOR'S ASSESSMENT

CHARITY CYCLIST'S TRAGIC DEATH

Banned from the major television channels for several years after a series of drink-drugs-sex scandals, Dave Delaney, **the former child star-turned disc jockey** had accepted the challenge to cycle from John O'Groats to **Lands End** to raise funds for a children's charity. The idea was to prove he was now 'clean' in mind and body, a man of compassion.

But he was already two days behind schedule on his **1,000-mile** mission and the previous evening his business manager had phoned to say his sponsors were beginning to worry that he would not meet the plan for his arrival at a children's hospital near **Lands End** to be screened live on a peak-time TV programme.

When his support riders had stopped that morning to take on water from a roadside fountain, Delaney had slipped into the village pub, grabbed a bottle of Coke and a **Brandy** and drank from both, complaining his 'guts felt queer'. A couple of hours later, he was seen furtively swallowing a handful of white pills – 'my little white clouds,' he cheerfully explained.

Punctuation

Land's End takes an apostrophe

Heading

Without a verb, this is more of a label than a heading – reminiscent of a local newspaper's report of a road accident. Lacks drama. Many deaths are tragic.

Punctuation

The phrase 'the former child star-turned disc jockey' diverts from the main flow of the sentence to explain who David Delaney is. Needs to begin and end with a comma.

Accuracy

His mission is not 1,000 miles long. Distance from John O'Groats to Land's End is given as 874 miles using main roads and bridges but cyclists make use of minor roads, totalling 814 miles.

Grammar

As an abbreviation of a proprietary brand, Coke carries a capital letter but brandy is a generic term and does not.

Nearing the top of a steep ascent on a bleak Lancashire moor, his bike suddenly went into a zig-zag, pitching him on to a rocky bank. **When Dave Delaney's limp body was pulled from his bike, his fingers had to be pealed from the handlebars one by one – the death-grip agony of massive cardiac failure in his desperate effort to revive a once glittering career.**

The first to reach him found his face turning yellow, his eyes bulging. **Mouth to mouth** and chest massage produced nothing but a drawn-out bubbling from his lungs, the smell of brandy still on his breath.

A local doctor rushing to the scene pronounced him dead. Pulling up the rider's jersey to examine the body, two more tubes of white amphetamine pills were revealed. Shaking his head, the doctor murmured: 'Drink and drugs; a crazy mix.'

But David Delaney was well aware of the risk hidden in his little white clouds. He had no choice but to die in the attempt to resurrect a career long dead.

The last words on that remote hillside from a voice which once commanded audiences of millions had been: **'Its** all right. Get me back on my bike. I want to go on …'

Structure

This sentence would make a better intro.

Spelling

'pealed' refers to bells; should be 'peeled' as in taking the skin off an orange. Spell-check would not signal this mistake.

Punctuation

Mouth to mouth needs to be hyphenated as it is a single unit defining the technique.

Grammar

The first sentence of this paragraph suggests the doctor pronounced him dead while rushing to the scene. In reality, it was 'A local doctor, who rushed to the scene, pronounced him dead.'

The second sentence illustrates a common error. Opening with a qualifying clause is a good way to vary a sequence of sentences comprising Subject-Verb-Object of 'The cat sat on the mat' variety. The BBC style book refers to these as 'danglers' but it must be the Subject which is dangled. Here, the strict interpretation is that it was the tubes of pills which pulled up the rider's jersey.

Punctuation

A semicolon denotes a pause greater than a comma in adding elements to the principal message of the sentence. Here, we needed a colon because it marks a step forward, linking cause with effect. Henry Watson Fowler, legendary authority on English usage, described the colon as 'delivering the goods that have been invoiced in the preceding words.'

Structure

Would make a better ending.

Punctuation

Its takes an apostrophe – an abbreviation of 'It is'. Delaney already dead earlier in the story.

THE SUBBED VERSION – READY FOR PRESS

LITTLE WHITE CLOUDS SHATTER THE COMEBACK DREAM

When Dave Delaney's limp body was pulled from his bike on a bleak Lancashire moor, his fingers had to be peeled from the handlebars one by one – the death-grip agony of massive cardiac failure in his desperate effort to revive a once glittering career.

Banned from the major television channels for several years after a series of drink-drug-sex scandals, the former child star-turned disc jockey had accepted the challenge to cycle from John O'Groats to Land's End to raise funds for a children's charity. The idea was to prove he was now 'clean' in mind and body, and a man of compassion.

But he was already two days behind schedule on his 814-mile mission and the previous evening his business manager had phoned to say his sponsors were beginning to worry that he would not meet the plan for his arrival at a children's hospital near Land's End to be screened live on a peak-time TV programme.

When his support riders had stopped that morning to take on water from a roadside fountain, Delaney had slipped into a village pub, grabbed a bottle of Coke and

Headings benefit from action words – crash, jump, scream, die ... Here we have **action** – 'shatter' – plus **imagery** – 'little white clouds' – and **intrigue** – who's having what sort of comeback shattered? While news headlines bring together the main facts of the story, feature headings tend to seek to invoke atmosphere.

The reader is immediately plunged into the heart of the story, there is the wide-angle shot of the bleak landscape and then a zooming into the close-up of the fingers being peeled from the handlebars. The comeback is explained by 'his desperate effort to revive a once glittering career'.

The original intro now placed to identify the central character and provides hard information about his mission. No second comma needed after 'child star-turned disc jockey' because, with Delaney already named, this phrase is now the subject of the sentence and must not be separated from its verb

This para now established the timing of the incident and the need for Delaney to take drastic action to meet his sponsors' demands.

one of brandy and drank from both, complaining his 'guts felt queer'. A couple of hours later, he was seen furtively swallowing a handful of white pills – 'my little white clouds,' he cheerfully explained.

Nearing the top of a steep ascent, his bike suddenly went into a zig-zag, pitching him on to a rocky bank. The first to reach him found his face turning yellow, his eyes bulging. Mouth-to-mouth and chest massage produced nothing but a drawn-out bubbling from his lungs, the smell of brandy still on his breath.

The last words on that remote hillside from a voice that once commanded audiences of millions were: 'It's all right. Get me back on my bike. I want to go on …'

A local doctor, who rushed to the scene, pronounced him dead and in pulling up the rider's jersey to examine the body found two more tubes of white amphetamine pills. Shaking his head, the doctor murmured: 'Drink and drugs: a crazy mix.'

But David Delaney was well aware of the risk hidden in his little white clouds. He had no choice but to die in the attempt to resurrect a career long dead.

Originally left to the end of the original copy, this para is more effective linked to the smell of brandy on his dying breath.

Much better to conclude with a poignant link with the 'little white clouds' of the Heading. Topping and tailing makes for a satisfying read – no loose ends.

Not only will a full understanding of the sub-editor's craft enhance the writer's personal output, it is a vital step towards any ambition of becoming a commissioning editor and perhaps ultimately acquiring the editor's chair.

14 Make the Photographer Your Friend

The writer producing words that make pictures destined primarily for the page must be aware that the extent to which those words are read and enjoyed will largely depend on one thing – actual pictures printed on the page and the way they are displayed

As previously explained, it is pictures which pull readers into a page and the writer should therefore take this into account in shaping the story. The more the content throws up visual images, the greater the scope for illustration on the page.

This is where the writer's choice of location for an interview can be crucial – a cliff-top setting for that interview with a lifeboat coxswain has so much more potential than a chat in his favourite pub. Better still if the encounter can be staged at sea in the course of a rescue mission.

In the past, many journalists preferred to work apart from photographers. They saw each other as different species. The journalist found the clicking of cameras as intruding on the intimacy he was trying to achieve with his subject; the photographer chose to do his own thing, making a personal choice of the most pleasing image to an artistic eye.

Working to achieve the same message

The result was that the pictures on the page often failed to reflect the message of the print. That will not happen if the writer makes the photographer his friend and an active collaborator. Not only can the journalist provide a first-hand briefing on the main thrust of his piece, the photographer having his own needs might come up with another choice for a location offering him the most dramatic possibilities.

Both are seeking maximum exposure in their newspaper or magazine. The more graphic the main illustration, the more readers will be tempted into the feature. But in seeking to achieve this partnership it is important for the writer to have a sympathetic understanding of a thinly disguised truth:

As a breed, photographers are basically neurotic – twice over.

The first cause is that they live with a fear of mechanical failure. They capture their pictures via a camera and a camera is a machine that can go wrong.

Back in the late 60s, a highly experienced photographer accompanied me on a seven-week tour of the Far East in which we

The writer and photographer need to be active collaborators if each is to attain his objective

hired a sampan to witness boat people fleeing Red China to find sanctuary in Hong Kong, rode in the helicopter of a flying doctor serving remote islands in the South China Sea, swam among the bare-breasted pearl divers of Kyoto, attended a memorial service for long-lost nuclear victims in Hiroshima, took part in a water festival where thousands of candles mounted on palm leaves floated through the heart of Bangkok, watched the leg-paddling canoeists of Northern Burma show off their racing skills and were relieved to have an armed escort as we passed through bandit country on an Irrawaddy paddle-steamer.

All of it wonderful spectacle for the photographer to capture – and in those pre-digital days each episode required us to rush to the nearest airport to get rolls of his precious film and a package of my typewritten copy back to our London office.

Nearing the end of the trip, a messenger entered the government rest house where we were staying in a jungle clearing outside Mandalay. In my imagination I like to think of him in a loin cloth and carrying a cleft stick but I have to confess he was a uniformed porter from a nearby hotel and he handed a rather crumpled telegram to the photographer.

It was originally addressed to him at the Imperial Hotel in Tokyo but we had clearly left before it arrived and so had been forwarded to where we stayed in Kyoto only to miss us there – as was to happen in being sent on its way successively to Hiroshima, Taiwan, Thailand and finally Burma.

The message was simple: 'Check camera immediately. All pictures blank since Hong Kong.'

My abiding memory of that most colourful jaunt around the Far East is of the physical degeneration of my photographer into a sobbing wreck who refused any consolation all the way back home and was never quite the same man again.

As a true professional, he had dutifully checked his camera every morning but had been equipped with a new Hasselblad for the trip, an advanced type of camera for its day with which he was unfamiliar and which happened to have an intricate shutter device. That did not respond to a routine check.

In our age of the digital camera he would have been able to check and edit his pictures after each shot. In our age of digital transmission he would have had no need for those dashes to the airport and merely sent the lot by email.

But the photographer's fear of mechanical failure is ever-present. Digital cameras can get damaged or lost; batteries can fail; hefty email

Why a wonderful spectacle eluded the efforts of a diligent photographer

Even intrepid war photographer Don McCullin would admit to working under what he termed the 'phantom of fear' – not referring to the hazards of the battlefield but the constant fear shared by all photograhers of their cameras letting them down or their arriving on the scene too late to catch the crucial moment

attachments can mysteriously disappear into the ether.

And even when the equipment and communications work perfectly, the photographer has a secondary neurosis – the fear of not being there when something special happens. The photographer records moments in time and if he is not there those moments have gone forever. They cannot be re-staged.

Summing up a long Fleet Street career, photographer Harry Benson defines his profession by citing a poem written by Robert Louis Stevenson in 1885 called *From a Railway Carriage Window*.

'He's looking out,' says Benson and he sees a boy gathering brambles, a cart in the road. The last line is "Each a glimpse and gone forever!"

'That's the kind of photography I like. A good photograph is gone. It can never happen again.'

Or could have been missed by a couple of seconds. Benson admits to having nightmares about how the tiniest lapse of timing or indecision could have cost him some of his most celebrated pictures – capturing the anguish of Ethel Kennedy just moments after the assassination of her husband Robert, catching Donald Trump using one of the world's first car phones while riding through New York in his limousine in 1981, happening upon the youthful Beatles indulging in an exuberant pillow fight in a Paris hotel room (an image in *Time* magazine's list of the 100 most influential photos of all time).

When Benson lies awake and thinks about such pictures the nightmare is that he might not have been on the spot to take them.

Eye-witnesses can reconstruct the scene

Writers are fortunate. If they are not there, the event can be re-constructed in words by interviewing people who were there. I would have hated to miss any of the highlights of our Asian journeyings but in no case would it have been a total disaster. Eye-witnesses would have been available in plenty. I could have revisited the scene the next day.

With every smartphone a digital camera, the journalist and the photographer are now often the same person. Which gives the writer complete control over the package so long as in planning words that make pictures in the mind he ensures that those words project real-life situations that his camera can capture.

As the written word of the twenty-first century is mostly transferred to a website, he will take care to shoot video since moving pictures bring live action to the screen.

But to achieve maximum impact on the page he needs to be looking for the most arresting moment that can be captured in a single shot.

Far from being inferior to moving pictures, the still picture can often lay claim to more memorable effect in that it can freeze and encapsulate a defining moment.

The still picture lodges in our mind

While the human brain finds it difficult to select and replay crucial sequences from many hours of film or TV coverage of momentous events, a still picture can lodge in our minds for an eternity.

Out of all the bloody years of the Vietnam wars, we tend to recall that one shot of the scorched body of a naked child fleeing from a napalm attack; amid all the horrors of D-Day we recall the moment when a landing craft dropped its ramp and young soldiers first stared at the hostile shore awaiting them.

Whether historic or personal, tragic or amusing, our heads contain many such snapshots: the troubled life of Princess Diana captured as a lonely figure in front of the Taj Mahal, in forlorn contrast with that monument to undying love ... Jackie Kennedy cradling the shattered head of the mortally wounded President ... The Beatles in their pomp striding across a pedestrian crossing ... Twiggy symbolising the fashion revolution of the 60s by posing in an A-line mini-dress and Courreges boots ... the London bobby defending public decency by using his helmet to shield the private parts of Twickenham's first streaker ...

The art of creative cropping

'Anyone who can replay moving images in his mind has a rare faculty,' wrote Harold Evans in the introduction to his book, *Pictures on a Page* (Pimlico). 'The moving image may make an emotional impact, but its detail and shape cannot easily be recalled.'

Equipped with a digital camera or smartphone, a writer can edit his pictures on the spot by being able to review each shot and adjust accordingly.

As Editor of *The Times* and *Sunday Times*, Evans was a passionate advocate of the art of 'creative cropping' – the recognition of that portion within a picture that is its main story, framing the image to exclude extraneous detail.

Very often, that follows the path of TV's zoom lens and closes in on the heart of the image.

Deciding how closely to crop has been described as looking for the story within the picture

Cropping is not always zooming in close to the heart of the picture. Sometimes the bigger story demands a wider view

For example, the subject is a middle-aged business executive, balding and bespectacled, having protruding ears and wearing a spotted tie with a dark grey suit. Pictured as a head-and-shoulders shot, he is hardly worth a second look.

But with the top of the image cropped to above his eyeline (losing the bald pate), cropped into his cheeks (no protruding ears), and cropped up to his chin (losing his jowls and sight of the suit and tie), he can appear positively dynamic. You are looking into his eyes.

As a general rule, the tighter the crop, the more impact. But Evans warns that the real story of the scene may lie wider than that.

Return of the wounded warrior

He gives two examples in his book (acclaimed as the bible of journalistic photography):
*   A couple are photographed embracing at the edge of an expanse of airport runway. He is a soldier returned from the war, being welcomed back by his wife. The temptation is to trim out as much as possible of that expanse of grey concrete and close in tightly on the two figures to highlight the moment of their joyful reunion. But that would lose an element which brings poignancy to the scene. Lying on the ground, two or three yards behind the soldier, is a crutch – the warrior has returned with only one leg!
*   Helping to contain devastating flooding of the Mississippi, a file of American convicts are shown stooped under the weight of the sandbags carried over their shoulders as they help to strengthen a threatened levee. Cropped to knee-length to emphasize this physical body strain, the picture suggests selfless convicts eager to make a contribution for the common good. Shown full length, they would be seen to be manacled together at their ankles. The 'willing volunteers' are members of a chain gang!

Creatively cropped, a picture is certain to catch the eye, but to hold the attention it must be accompanied by a caption answering the question that the image brings to mind.
*   Why is that woman looking so sad?
*   Why is that coach dangling on the edge of a precipice?
*   Why is that astronaut outside the spaceship?

Only when the caption answers such questions will the reader be persuaded to turn to the heading, grasp the subject of the story and be inclined to start reading the main body of the text.

So a writer providing his own captions has every incentive to create

The Royal Navy performed the changing of the guard outside Buckingham Palace yesterday – a first in the drill's 357-year history Photograph: Simon Dawson/Reuters

From all the bustle of the pomp and ceremony marking the Royal Navy taking over the guard at Buckingham Palace for the first time, the *Guardian* chose to close in on one figure to demonstrate that a woman was now standing guard over the Queen.

Watershed moment **The Royal Navy stepped in to perform Changing the Guard at Buckingham Palace yesterday for the first time in the ceremony's 357-year history**

The Times chose to take in a slightly wider shot – showing **two** figures to contrast the modest proportions of the female guard with the towering stature of the more traditional sentinel. The picture thus becomes a study in gender.

the strongest reasons for the reader completing that sequence and going on to read his precious story. Thus:

- A young mother driven to suicide by a shadow from her past
- The school outing hi-jacked by terrorists
- Space mission's race against time to fix re-entry problems.

Too often, captions merely identify what is pictured. The best captions add to what you see in the picture.

For example, suppose the only illustration made available for a business story on the annual report of a major corporation is a head-and-shoulders photograph of the kind of dull, middle-aged businessman previously described. We have demonstrated how creative cropping can turn him into a dynamic figure but that will have only passing appeal if merely captioned as:

Arnold Bloggs, CEO of Fremantle Enterprises.

How much more intriguing if the caption reads: Arnold Bloggs, CEO of Fremantle Enterprises – a man with a million worries.

There is an immediate compulsion to go into the story and find out what these worries are.

Such is the power of photographs and their captions to gain the reader's attention. This may leave young writers feeling that the text is relegated to the end of the food chain. Not at all. The whole point of the visual elements of magazine and newspaper design is to deliver an audience for the overriding objective of the process – getting the story read.

And Michael Deacon, a Parliamentary sketch writer for the *Daily Telegraph*, argues that those same words can show you things a camera can't:

> A photographer can show you politician Nigel Farage holding a pint of beer and grinning. That's about it. A writer, on the other hand, can show you him swaggering into the room, squelching with glee, and sporting that mischievous bug-eyed smirk that makes him look like a toad plotting a practical joke. The words don't just tell you what their subject looks like; they capture his character, his temperament, his mood, his essence.
>
> This is why I'll always prefer written journalism to TV or video. I'd rather read a good description of an event than watch footage of it. The pictures are better.

Who could deny the leading role of pictures in dominating layouts if they open up the world where words can create their own kind of pictures?

Pictures gain enormously by carrying captions which add more than what can be seen

Words can go further than pictures by capturing the mood and manner of the subject

15 Making Sure It's Read

As attention spans are inclined to shrink in a multimedia world, presentation is the key to a journalist's work reaching its intended audience. And with digital material accessed via the smaller screens of smartphones and tablets, the printed page seeks to exploit its extra size by employing a variety of techniques to engage the reader

The big difference between words meant for the page and words put on screen is that the latter are constructed to contain signposts to all the extra elements that are available online, offering various opportunities to divert from the text and bring the story to life by way of vox-pop interviews, video clips, animated graphics, background statistics, cross-references to relevant contemporary items and to any available archive footage.

It's like following a route through a countryside rich in tourist attractions, feeling free to turn off and follow signposts to explore whatever catches the eye before returning to the main road and going on to reach the final destination.

Words in print set out to achieve the very opposite, tailored as a seamless garment to give no inclination to divert.

It's more like a journey by rail with each paragraph linked to the one in front, staying firmly on track and leaving the passengers to enjoy the scenery by way of images provided from within the words. A vivid anecdote can match the impact of a video clip, a colourful quote can be more telling than a vox-pop, an imaginative analogy as revealing as a pie-chart, the past captured in a simple change of tense. There should be no need to go anywhere else: this is the complete package.

One other distinction is the matter of size. Where once the laptop was the natural home for online material, more and more people now choose to access by tablet or smartphone. This means limited opportunity for display through sheer lack of space. Compared to what can be seen on a tablet, a double-page spread in an A4 magazine is wide-screen TV; compared to what can be seen on a hand-held smartphone, a tabloid newspaper spread suggests i-MAX cinema.

Whereas presentation on the small screen accepts its confines and is essentially functional, magazine and newspaper designers have the space to exploit a whole range of so-called page furniture – headings, sub-headings, standfirsts, straplines, captions, pull-quotes, sidebars and panels (all of which are demonstrated on the following pages). Additionally they can call upon typefaces of vast variety to give added texture to the pages.

But central to all this is the single picture which dominates the layout, creatively cropped and used big. This is the keystone of the layout. Until it is in position further design cannot take place. There may be other pictures on a spread but this one must loom large. All other elements are assembled around this focal point

Research shows that it is the big picture which makes the passing reader stop and engage with the page. Next is the caption which explains the significance of the picture. Perhaps surprisingly, only then is the heading taken into account. With interest thus aroused, the reader moves on to the standfirst which must further excite this interest and so leads on to an intro which makes a compelling start to the body text.

Big picture, caption, heading, standfirst, intro – five stages on the way to performing the ultimate task of a layout – getting the story read.

Much of the above might be deemed to be the preserve of the designer. But by understanding the methodology behind the layout the writer can ensure he delivers the lively ingredients the designer requires. Above all – whether overseeing a photographer or operating as his own cameraman – providing that big picture.

Only when the big picture is chosen can the rest of the layout be assembled

Big picture caption

Strap

Eating for 14 hours at a stretch, an elephant consumes over three tons of food a day – and if still hungry will eat wood from whole branches wrenched from trees

While elephants hunted for their tusks are in danger of extinction in other parts of Africa, Botswana's ruthless policy of shooting ivory poachers on sight is creating a very different problem

GENTLE GIANTS
or
RAMPAGING MONSTERS?

Heading

Desperate measures may be needed to control the numbers of a creature seemingly capable of heart-rending grief at the loss of its baby and yet capable of wreaking mass destruction on an entire environment

Standfirst

Intro

The kill was before first light. The funeral took place that afternoon. A lioness, returning empty-bellied from a nocturnal prowl in Botswana's Chobe National Park, spotted a baby elephant separated from its herd in the night and walking uncertainly along a shallow valley.

Her muzzle and pale stomach only inches from the ground, her tawny coat almost invisible in the grey gloom, the lioness made its feline stalk to within 15 metres downwind of its prey – then exploded into a rush and pounce. Claws sank into the elephant's neck, pulling it to the ground, jaws tearing open the exposed throat. The baby elephant would have died without a whimper.

Over the next two hours, the lioness enjoyed a leisurely breakfast, watched by her three cubs hidden in a grove of the woolly caper bush overlooking the valley. Only when she exchanged places with them, allowing three smaller mouths to explore the crimson tunnel she had made into the carcass, was there activity from the surrounding trees.

All morning a growing assembly of vultures had flown into view, lining every bough, necks sunken, eyes fixed on the small mountain of flesh. Now they took to the air and paraglided into a semi-circle around the dead elephant, landing gaitered feet first, wings unfurled to the span of a boastful fisherman, then promptly folded tight as an umbrella.

Undeterred, the cubs continued tearing out flesh from within the armoured hide. They

Deep caption

Running head

Pullquotes

Do elephants really have the capacity for sorrow?

Botswana's 120,000 elephants march through the African bush like an army of World War 1 tanks – leaving behind a swathe of World War 1 destruction –tottered trees left leafless, limbless and splintered, the stricken landscape littered with piles of their half-brick-sized dung like battlefield debris

chewed on even when the more daring of the vultures, pink-faced and white-legged, began to edge forward to join in the feast.

This was the signal for the lioness to erupt from the bushes and drive them 20 – 30 metres back in a flurry of wings. But no sooner had she returned to the shade and the cubs resumed their meal than the vultures advanced once more -- prompting the lioness to give them another warning dash This weary process was repeated several times during the morning but when the noonday sun was blazing into its fiercest heat, the cubs suddenly retreated to their mother and the vultures returned to the trees, leaving the tempting dish unattended.

A dark mound had appeared above the horizon, followed by another, then another and another, all heading in this direction. As they grew closer we could see a

Lions hiding in the bushes watched the scene of their kill with great oval eyes, unblinking

column of elephants, headed by their matriarch, the grandmother (or even great-grandmother) of the herd, her tattered ears indicating great age.

On they came, until they began to assemble around the bloody remains of the baby elephant, some stamping their feet and snorting in the direction of the lion family they knew still to be near. But most would lightly touch and sniff the body with their trunks and then move to a respectable distance, standing in silent groups.

Still more elephants arrived until there were at least a hundred in all, the latecomers filtering their way to the body,

seemingly paying their respects, then moving to the rear of the congregation.

All the time the lions watched from the shade of the bushes, great oval eyes unblinking – perhaps like terrorists relishing the extent of the grief they had caused without ever being able to comprehend the depth of that grief.

Then the matriarch abruptly turned away and began to head back along the valley. Others followed until only one female was left. Our Botswanan guide was certain it would be the mother. She took a last look at the body, then moved down the slope to where she scented the actual kill had taken place. There she straddled the spot, urinated and defecated, then brushed dust over the small mound she had created.

Finally, she half-raised her trunk in the direction of the lions – more in dismissal than protest, leaving the carcass for them to gorge and the vulture to pick clean.With that, she joined on the doleful procession, now stretching as far as the eye could see, heads lowered, moving trunk to tail in a stately slow march.

So we had experienced the rare spectacle of an elephant funeral.

Or had we? Weren't we investing a primeval animal with human feelings? Were we mistaking their natural solemnity for a formal display of grief? Do elephants really have the capacity for sorrow?

In a paper for the Journal of Applied Animal Behaviour, Iain Douglas Hamilton, founder of Save The Elephants, wrote: "The question of whether there might be emotional or mental suffering among surviving

elephants who encounter and interact with ailing or dead elephants is open, but behavioural data suggests this is the case."

What's difficult to reconcile with this image of caring creatures is the way an army of elephants marches through the African bush with the ponderous progression of World War 1 tanks. Unfortunately, their frequent advances leave behind a swathe of World War 1 destruction – tottered trees left leafless, limbless and splintered, the stricken landscape littered with piles of their half-brick sized dung like battlefield debris.

We had experienced the rare spectacle of an elephant funeral. But had we?

Eating for 14 hours at a stretch, an elephant consumes 325kgs of food a day. When leaves and fruit fail to fill that giant stomach, it tears off whole branches and eats the wood. Its tusks gouge so much bark from around the stems of full grown trees that turn into whitened skeletons and eventually fall at dizzy angles. Trees that survive are pushed sideways to the ground so that their roots can be munched.

Now numbering one for every 14 human inhabitants, the relentless

> **Republic of Botswana – former British protectorate, declared independent September 30, 1966. Population: 2,029, 307. Area: 224,610 square miles.**

roaming of Botswana's 120,000 elephants is driving villagers from the land by indiscriminatingly destroying their crops. Even the staunchest conservationists now concede some significant culling is necessary

One proposal is to deplete their numbers by taking out the juvenile members of a herd. Having witnessed the display of grief over the death of one baby, it is disturbing to imagine the degree of communal trauma at any systematic slaughter of the young.

An alternative is to cull a percentage of the elders. But this would shatter the social hierarchy of the herd in which age is revered and the adults are responsible for the upbringing and disciplining of the young – especially teenage bulls.

"The only realistic way to make any sizeable reduction in numbers," says game camp manager Bob Flaxman, "is to take out a whole herd at one go. That would be the cleanest and kindest method - with no survivors left to grieve or go wild. But are we ready to go that far?"

If UK animal rights activists were driven to mount overnight commando raids on a tiny Scottish island to rescue hedgehogs under threat of culling, it's not difficult to calculate the degree of world-wide fury at what would be seen to be wholesale massacre of these gentle giants.

For regardless of the urgent need to limit the massive damage they are clearly inflicting on their

"Thank you for saving my baby"

Safari lodge manager Bob Flaxman went to the rescue when he came across a baby elephant trapped in a marsh while her mother watched helplessly from dry land. Reversing his Landrover to the edge of the quagmire, Flaxman took a cable from his power winch, waded out to the stricken creature, managed to loop the cable around its shoulders, then struggled back to his vehicle and was able to slowly winch the baby to safety.

"Elephants are very defensive of their young ," says Flaxman, "and the mother, already very agitated, began to stamp the ground and adopt an aggressive stance when I first arrived on the scene. Then she saw what I was trying to do and waited patiently while I managed the rescue.

"Afterwards she turned to me and gently wiped the mud from my clothes with her trunk – as if to say: 'Thank you for saving my baby'.

"To my mind, there is no doubt that elephants do have emotions very much like ours."

Pullquotes

Fact box

Panel/sidebar

Heading
There is a school of thought which believes Headings should always be positive and therefore never carry a question mark. But this is not possible when the feature addresses an issue of divided attitudes. The advantage of posing a question is that it achieves a measure of interactivity (a vital dimension of this digital age). The reader is challenged to come inside the feature, to assess the evidence and then to form a personal opinion. Involvement is complete.

Big picture caption
Adds to what we see of the giant image looming out of the page – fascinating information on an elephant's appetite – eating 14 hours

a day, consuming three tons of food, including whole branches wrenched from trees. Very much a 'Who would believe it?' nugget to be relayed to astounded acquaintances.

Strap
Sets out the main ingredients of the story. If transferred from print to the screen meets the need for SEOs (Search Engine Optimisation) – elephants/Africa/Botswana/ivory poachers.

Standfirst (so called because it is the most prominent piece of copy, positioned to lead into the body of the text)
This is essentially a piece of advertising copy, selling the story in the most dramatic terms – much as the blurb on the back of a paperback novel ('A gripping tale of passion and treachery within a tropical paradise haunted by memories of a tragic romance.') This is not an area for genteel restraint. Here we have 'desperate measures'/'heart-rending grief'/'wreaking mass destruction'…

Intro
The impact of the big picture plus the salesmanship of the Strap, Heading and Standfirst should lead the reader into the opening of the body text but here, too, the challenge is to further engage the attention: 'The kill was before first light. The funeral took place that afternoon.' Who would not want to read on?

Running head
Having won the attention of readers with the opening spread, the Running head on the turn pages is intended to encourage them to stay with the story – in this case by adding to the question posed by the main heading on the preceding spread.

Deep caption
More information to add to the picture and a vivid analogy of a World War battlefield created by an army of elephants. And we now learn there are 120,000 of them.

Pullquotes
These serve two purposes. First to break up otherwise solid columns of type and so provide an assurance that the story is going to be easy to read. Second they are another form of 'selling' the contents to the passing customer. Prominently displayed and easily able to catch the

The target is the 'twin-track' reader who flicks through the pages looking for self-contained smaller items which are interesting enough to tempt them to go back and read the whole feature

eye, these mentions of lions watching their kill with 'great oval eyes unblinking' and of whether or not these giant creatures have 'the capacity for sorrow' provide yet more reasons for going back to read the whole feature.

Panel/sidebar

The challenge is to persuade readers to stay with a long feature and so this second Spread contains what is in effect a short story within the story – 'Thank you for saving my baby'. There is a fresh element to absorb but one which naturally springs from the main narrative.

This device is also very much of the twin-track approach of design in seeking to catch the attention of a would-be reader merely flicking through a magazine by providing self-contained and easily digestible items on otherwise run-of-paper pages. Someone pausing briefly to read 'Thank you for saving my baby' might be tempted to go back to the beginning of the feature and read the whole thing.

Fact box

A useful device for presenting a series of hard facts of background information (location, area, population etc) which might spoil the flow of the story if incorporated in the main text. Adds authority to the feature and provides another point of interest on the page.

Long or short, headings should conjure up images and situations that both attract and intrigue

Jaw-dropping risks behind perfect smile

Dentists warn of dangers of extreme dental procedures, dubbed 'porcelain pornography' – often at considerable cost to health and wealth

The Day of the Dead comes to life

Mexican children's film of a battle for lost souls

I, er, yuh um ...crikey

Interview with a bumbling Boris Johnson

HOW CLEVER IS YOUR DOG?

Quiz to assess whether a dog's intelligence is due to breeding or intensive training – stories about pets always pull in the readers

Fracking: the explosive truth

Warning to Government that 40 of the seats the Tories most want to win in a General Election are in areas they have opened up for fracking

Lazy days beside the world's most beautiful lagoon

Armchair travellers will readily respond to an exotic feature on the South Seas island that provoked the infamous mutiny on the Bounty

Profile of UKIP's first Member of Parliament

'They've watched *Love Actually* and think it's a manual for how to govern the country'

Woman columnist recommends a children's doll as a role model for career women thinking of delaying motherhood

Freeze your eggs? Ladies, ask yourselves what Barbie would do

How to turn your commute into a date with destiny

It's easy to find love on a train, says the 'Subway Romeo' who claims to have dated 500 women he happened to meet on New York's subway

Turn pages need boldly displayed pullquotes otherwise the passing reader will keep on turning

The locals remembered him as bright, dissatisfied and rude: a child who blew pepper into a teacher's face and was given to picking fights

He placed the head inside two plastic shopping bags, wound the hands in grocery bags and the torso in plastic sheets

Story of a small-town boy who grew up to be a New York banker – who led a double life as chainsaw murderer

'We dived forward. We hit the sandbar. It was surreal – I couldn't move. I was lying in a star shape'

'It's like a death. I wake up and sometimes, for a split second, you forget. Then it's hard'

A young man tells of his struggles to come to terms with life after the swimming accident that severed his spinal cord

'IF THE WORLD WERE GAY, I DON'T THINK BUILDERS WOULD BE WOLF-WHISTLING ME'

'IT'S THE GANGS,' WHISPERS MY HONDURAN SHAMPOO LADY. 'IF THEY DON'T JOIN, THEY GET KILLED'

Confessions of a famous TV presenter who revealed that he was homosexual

A woman journalist is sent to investigate the trafficking of children across the US–Mexican border

'GUILT AND FEAR BECAME A PART OF YOU, SOMETHING YOU CAN'T SHAKE. I WAS TERRIFIED OF GROWING UP, TERRIFIED OF MEN'

'I THINK I WOULD BE SICK IF I SAW HIM. I'D WANT TO PUNCH HIS LIGHTS OUT. I AM STILL AFRAID OF HIM'

Case histories of former victims exposing the years of child abuse they suffered at a church boarding school

HE HAS THIS MANNER THAT NEW CELEBRITIES FIND IMPOSSIBLE TO AFFECT – HE SEEMS TOTALLY OPEN WITHOUT TELLING YOU ANYTHING

An interview with David Beckham

Principles of Design

- Anything complicated, confusing, messy or simply dull will not succeed

- People respond to pictures more quickly than to words so a dominant image will pull the reader in

- One big picture is the most effective but a layout can work if two or three pictures are brought together into an overall unit

- The first step to a layout is to position the main image. This is the keystone of the page(s). Everything else – supporting pictures, heading, standfirst and body text – are arranged to support the main image

- The number of supporting pictures will depend upon the amount of text to get in. But since the visual appeal of the page is paramount it may be necessary to cut the text to fit

- Every picture must carry a caption since while readers react first to pictures they immediately want to know what the image represents

- Captions should not be a mere label but must ADD to what is seen in the picture. E.g. a shot of AFC Bournemouth's ground could be captioned thus:
  Home of the Cherries – success on the field but financial worries in the boardroom

- Since a single page of editorial has to compete with a facing advertisement, designers value the chance to layout double-page spreads (DPS in the business) and want to take advantage of the 'widescreen' dimensions

- This can only be achieved by visually linking the two pages horizontally and the most obvious way to achieve this is for the main image to spread across the gutter between the two pages

- All the supporting elements should also line up horizontally so that two smaller pictures or panels positioned at the outside bottom corners of the two pages should be of the same depth

- The effect is to stretch the apparent width of the spread to create

The first requirement of a layout is to catch the eye and stop the reader turning the page

the maximum impact. The two pages become a single unit

- If the first requirement is to stop the reader turning the page, that in turn leads to the most basic purpose of a layout:
  To make the reader want to read the words
  And the words must be easy to read!

- So beware of reversed-out type against a background colour or peeping through a complicated picture because every reader survey carried out by publishers shows that people most often can't be bothered to read it
     Used sparingly for a heading, a standfirst or a brief passage it can be most effective. Used for body text across a whole page or spread it defeats the whole object of making reading easy

If you must use reversed-out type there are three rules:
1. Go up in size and leading
2. Use a sans serif face
3. Set it bold

Now is the time for all good men to come to the aid of the party. Now is the time for all good men to come to the aid of the party. Now is the time for all good men to come to the aid of the party. Now is the time to come to the aid of the party.
Now is the time for all good men to come to the aid of the party. Now is the time for all good men to come to the aid of the party. Now is the time for all good men to come to the aid of the party. Now is the time to come to the aid of the party. Now is the time for all good men to come to the aid of the party. Now is the time for all good men to come to the aid of the party. Now is the time to come to the

10/13pt
Black ink/white paper – easy to read

Now is the time for all good men to come to the aid of the party. Now is the time for all good men to come to the aid of the party. Now is the time for all good men to come to the aid of the party. Now is the time to come to the aid of the party.
Now is the time for all good men to come to the aid of the party. Now is the time for all good men to come to the aid of the party. Now is the time for all good men to come to the aid of the party. Now is the time to come to the aid of the party. Now is the time for all good men to come to the aid of the party. Now is the time for all good men to come to the aid of the party. Now is the time for all good men to come to the aid of the party. Now is the time to come to the aid of the

10/13pt
Reversed-out black – more difficult to read

Now is the time for all good men to come to the aid of the party. Now is the time for all good men to come to the aid of the party. Now is the time for all good men to come to the aid of the party. Now is the time to come to the aid of the party. Now is the time for all good men to come to the aid of the party. Now is the time for all good men to come to the aid of the party. Now is the time for all good men to come to the aid of the party. Now is the time to come to the aid of the party. Now is the time for all good men to come to the aid of the party. Now is the time to come to

12/14pt
Bigger type – easier to read

Now is the time for all good men to come to the aid of the party. Now is the time for all good men to come to the aid of the party. Now is the time for all good men to come to the aid of the party. Now is the time to come to the aid of the party.

Now is the time for all good men to come to the aid of the party. Now is the time for all good men to come to the aid of the party. Now is the time for all good men to come to the aid of the party. Now is the time to come to the aid of the party. Now is the time to come to the aid of the party. Now is the time to come to the aid of the

12/14pt
Sans serif face – much easier to read

Now is the time for all good men to come to the aid of the party. Now is the time for all good men to come to the aid of the party. Now is the time for all good men to come to the aid of the party. Now is the time to come to the aid of the party. Now is the time for all good men to come to the aid of the party. Now is the time for all good men to come to the aid of the party. Now is the time for all good men to come to the aid of the party. Now is the time to come to the aid of the party. Now is the time to come to the aid of the party. Now is the time to come to the aid of the

12/14pt
Set bold – easiest to read

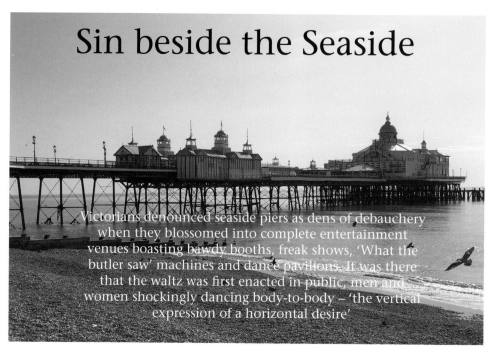

10/12pt
serif

Reversing-out type from a background picture needs to follow the same rule
of going up a size and switching to a sans serif face, set bold

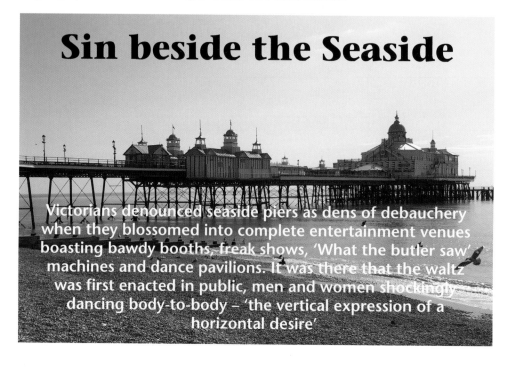

12/14pt
san serif
bold

16 Standing Out from the Crowd

Magazine covers can decide the success or failure of their publication.
No matter how many regular readers they may boast there is the need
to attract newcomers to make up for inevitable defections and, more
importantly, to win readers from their rivals

Accessing a magazine online merely involves calling up the
title and there it is on the screen in splendid isolation.
Coming across a magazine online in a moment of casual
browsing achieves the same result and offers immediate involvement.

A printed magazine has to fight for attention as one small element
in a crowded news-stand. For many years it was accepted that would-
be purchasers devoted only five to seven seconds in searching for
something to catch the eye; the latest research suggests that our
increasingly frenzied lifestyle has reduced that to no more than three
to five seconds.

In that fragment of time it is up to the cover to determine the
destiny of that issue. It is the crucial tool.

The cover is **not** the first page of editorial, **not** just a pretty picture,
not an elegant piece of design calculated to win media awards.

The cover's job is to **SELL, SELL, SELL.**

And above all, to sell itself to strangers – since faithful regular
readers will buy the magazine anyway – and to persuade lapsed readers
to come back home with the promise that this issue is more exciting
than when they decided 'It's not for me any more'.

Facing a double challenge

The more a cover projects a routinely familiar image the less likely it is
to dent that view. That is why the double challenge for a cover is to be
true to its brand and still offer the element of surprise that persuades
all those non-readers to come inside and have another look.

No matter how successful a title, it needs to replenish its readership
every issue to make up for the usual customers who happen to be
staying at home or travelling away, who are too busy with seasonal
shopping or have simply decided to buy something else. Or, rather
more basically, have died.

To that extent it is a recruitment poster.

It's the combination of imagery and words that makes for best-
selling covers. But it's the image that must dominate because it is what
first catches the eye; the words then provide reasons to buy.

The main cover-line is not just another headline transposed to

The bold image attracts
but the cover-lines
must deliver a selling
message

Too many items on a cover give it no chance of projecting itself as a recruitment poster

the front page; it has to be crafted as a sales slogan – advertising copy designed to excite, to challenge, to intrigue. Since advertising copywriters believe less is more, keep it short.

Research shows that having been attracted by a powerful cover shot linked with a compulsive cover-line, the casual buyer will only then take in the title logo and realize what magazine they have in their hand. If it's your magazine they're holding, congratulations – you have won a brand-new reader.

The cover then needs some further cover-lines to indicate the breadth and variety of content that lies inside. Ideally not more than four or five. Any more and the cover is merely listing routine ingredients instead of emphasizing what is special about this issue.

Unfortunately many publishers worried by falling sales in the face of digital opposition conspire to accelerate their own decline by choosing to pack their covers with as many items as possible – often smothering their main cover image with as many as 100 words of cover-lines and a multitude of smaller pictures and panels.

The result is they have no chance of being a recruitment poster. With a cover no more than a Contents page they have little hope of leaping out of that crowded news-stand.

A proud chef may be tempted to list every single ingredient of every single dish of his *a la carte* menu on a board outside his door in the hope of attracting passing trade. The reality is that if the restaurant doesn't look attractive at a glance you don't bother to cross the street to read all those words.

Advertisers are envious of covers' impact

Andy Rork, creative director of the Saatchi and Saatchi advertising empire in its heyday, specialized in media business, and in sitting in on ideas conferences of his client magazines was constantly surprised by the desultory manner in which covers were planned. If they were planned at all.

Often he found the cover being a last-minute press day choice of what was deemed to be the best picture already in the issue – with cover-lines being hastily cobbled together to justify the projection of that image.

'Any of my advertising clients,' Andy recorded, 'even faintly contemplating the unique privilege of his product occupying the front page of a publication reaching an audience often measured in

hundreds of thousands if not millions would be shocked to discover that many, if not most, magazine covers happen by chance.'

If the cover was to be a successful advertisement for the magazine, he argued, it had to be planned as an advertisement. That meant the first ideas conference of a new issue should not break up without deciding what upcoming element would not merely fill a few pages but would provide the most powerful reason to purchase, how compulsively that story could be best illustrated on the cover and what telling words would most strongly deliver a selling message.

Online magazines do not have the same challenge to stand out from the crowd because they are viewed in isolation. Increasingly seen on a small screen they do not have the physical impact of a successful printed cover which can transform the fortunes of its title by adding tens of thousands of sales through making best use of those three to five seconds at the news-stand.

In the highly competitive world of printed magazines the cover that can stand out from a crowded new-stand can add many, many thousands of extra sales

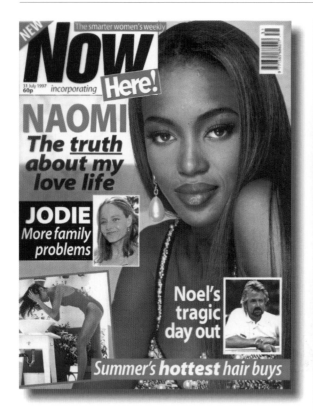

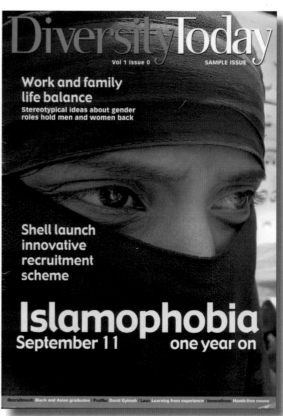

NOW magazine follows the classic formula of having a dominant image closely linked to its intriguing main cover-line while the supporting lines feature emotive words such as 'tragic', 'family problems', 'hottest'.

Lightly coloured covers are reckoned to be more attractive but *Diversity Today* (aimed at a specialist market) makes dramatic use of black to justify its cover girl wearing a burka behind that one-word cover-line – Islamophobia.

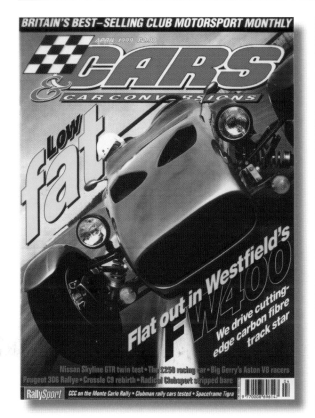

Motoring magazines face the difficulty that their covers naturally feature cars but a car is essentially a landscape object while covers are portrait. How to vary that constraint? *Cars and Car Conversions* is aimed at the go-faster audience and found this solution by tilting its head-on cover shot to create a strong sensation of speed.

Horse & Hound's Cheltenham preview hardly boasts snappy cover-lines but majors on single words that promise value for money – 'WIN', 'PLUS' and '32-page PULL-OUT'. The significance of this cover is that the horse is **looking to the right** – which should apply to any cover subject on any magazine – in that he is looking in a direction which suggests he is about to **go into the magazine**; looking left he would be **turning his back on the magazine**.

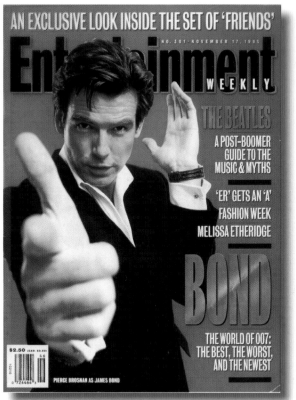

In seeking to leap out from that crowded news-stand, covers must seek to create a sense of interactivity with would-be purchasers. *Entertainment Week* certainly achieves this with an almost 3D shot of its cover star, with cover-lines linked to a single word that symbolizes a world of adventure: BOND – which then promises to tell 'THE BEST, THE WORST, AND THE NEWEST' of the world of 007. A package of superlatives.

Woman's Own achieves a more subtle sense of interactivity by featuring a pair of soap-opera stars on its cover but with the woman turning away from her unfaithful partner as if to confide in the readers just why 'The game's up, Ian!'

Eye contact is a key element in attracting engagement, as proved by the almost hypnotic World War One poster of Lord Kitchener declaring 'Your country needs YOU' – so successful that a whole generation volunteered for the killing fields of Flanders. Magazines' need for sales is less crucial but eye contact is sought in many ways. This *Harper's Bazaar* cover could have been a complete failure in that its spindly cover-lines were virtually unreadable but that almost witch-like pair of eyes would certainly attract attention. Blue eyes, blue logo, blue background create an overall effect that hardly needs cover-lines.

An Italian magazine, *iO*, preferred to create a monotone mood for their cover of Sharon Stone and the photogragher projects a sense of intimacy by shooting from an angle which suggests she is about to make intimate revelations.

If news-stands are heavily congested the last thing a cover needs if it is to be picked out from the crowd is to be overcrowded in itself. The women's weeklies market is fiercely competitive and many magazines make the mistake of thinking that the more items they offer on their covers they more they will be seen as offering most value for money.

This cover of *Chat* has not one but two cover girls, 13 smaller pictures and no less than 93 words of copy. In contrast, its principal rival, *Take a Break*, has one main image, eight smaller visuals and just six short and snappy over-lines: 'Clothes Cons EXPOSED'; 'Stop the WEDDING, Vicar!'; WOMEN WANT VIAGRA'; 'Stop JIGGING, floozy!'; 'Fun & FRUITY'; 'WIN £35,000.' Still a busy cover but much more punchy and controlled. Is it a coincidence that it was outselling *Chat* two to one?

With every magazine trying to produce the strongest cover picture on the news-stand there is always the chance to stand out by being very different through harnessing the power of mere words. In planning an issue on investors' fears of an economic recession, *Business Week* realized that money in itself is intangible as a cover subject and there was no one financier who could encapsulate a multi-stranded situation. Their answer was the shot of a hand with fingers crossed and the one word JITTERS spelled out in such a way as to appear jittery in itself. No single picture could have better communicated such a nervous world of finance.

TIME magazine faced a similar problem in covering the civil war in Rwanda. Pictures of desperate refugees, ruthless mercenaries, shell-shocked children and sobbing victims of rape were so prevalent as to have becomes clichés of this bloody conflict.

So what cover could symbolize all this? Here again *TIME* turned to words – and they said it all.

New Scientist is a remarkable publication in that its accuracy and authority is unquestioned and yet its reader-friendly approach means that as well as well as being a respected presence in laboratories and universities around the world it can sell in large quantities from the news-stand. This is due to heavy investment in cover design with original artwork being commissioned for its largely thematic issues. Knowing its readers have a pre-occupation with 'Big-Bang' theories (How did it happen? Why are we here?) this abstract illustration proclaims 'No time ... no space ... no thing' and then promises the magazine will explain what really happened on the day the Universe began'. Result: a best-selling issue.

So how to encompass all things Japanese when devoting a whole issue to the high-tech culture that is modern day Japan? Shots of Mount Fuji, flooded temple gates or the pearl-divers of Kyoto recall a very different era. The answer was the cheapest cover they have ever produced – a blob of red ink on a white background to suggest the flag of the Land of the Rising Sun, supported by no less than 10 intriguing cover-lines of no more than three words each: 'World's faster beer'; 'Life-giving fish'; Beating the Bullet'; 'Megabridges'; 'Examination hell'; Mile-high buildings'; 'Robot nurses'; 'Gadget City blues'; 'Green warriors'; 'High-tech condoms'.

In the quest for a successful formula, covers have been subjected to much research.

One finding is that cover-lines in upper-and-lowercase type are easier to read than caps in those three to five seconds. Witness slow-moving suburban traffic being directed by signposts with place names in caps while motorways employ lower case for destinations because they need to be read at high speed.

The reason is that looking at a signpost for, say, SHEFFIELD the brain has to identify each character in turn – S-H-E-F-F-I-E-L-D – and then assemble those nine characters into the name. On a motorway, destinations are quickly identified because when spelled out in upper-and-lower each one forms its own shape – the risers and descenders of the characters making up the name of Wolverhampton look different from those of Carlisle; Bridlington makes a very different shape from Birmingham.

This is not to say that caps must never be used in cover-lines but they should be reserved for the biggest, boldest cover-lines and kept short.

Another finding concerns readers' reaction to the choice of colours for covers:

- Red is seen as warm, able to project drama and excitement (not surprisingly the most-used colour on nearly all covers);
- Blue creates two reactions. Dark blue is seen as indicating quality. Light blue is seen as cold;
- Yellow is to be used sparingly because many people regard it as denoting cheapness. It is most effective when providing a stand-out yellow background to panels offering added value – special offers, free gifts, big money competitions;
- Green is to be avoided at all costs because in our supposedly rational world the superstition endures that it is the colour of bad luck. Even the readers of *New Scientist* turn away from green covers;
- White backgrounds are seen to make covers outgoing; dark backgrounds are recessive.

One other factor in determining the purchase of a magazine derives from the fascinating world of haptics.

H-A P-T-I-C-S – the science of touch.

Professor Chris Carr of the School of Textiles at the University of Manchester alerted the interest of both publishers and papermakers with his analysis of the motivation of women buying clothes.

LOOK ...TOUCH ... FEEL.

When a garment on the clothes-rack catches her eye, the shopper will go and pull it out then take the material between her fingers to assess the quality.

It's a question of shape when reading words and names at speed

For the casual reader the texture of a magazine gives a clue to value for money

Since the majority of readers across many fields of magazines are female this was not to be ignored since it replicates the process of choosing a magazine on the news-stand – spot it, pick it up, feel it, then decide if it's worth it.

As a tactile exercise, the weight and texture of the package can be a deciding factor. Thicker and glossier will appeal to the upmarket followers of fashion and lifestyle; slimmer and cheaper for followers of celebrity weeklies or hobby titles.

When the Italian fashion magazine *Grazia* was to be introduced into Britain as our first ever fashion **weekly,** the publishers went to great lengths to distinguish it from *Vogue*, glossiest of the glossy monthlies. Matching *Vogue* gloss for gloss would make it seem just another monthly which happened to come out weekly. Yet not matching *Vogue*'s air of luxury could have had the new magazine dismissed as a downmarket upstart.

Enter the world of papermakers and ink technologists. The result was the creation of a 'high, bright coated (silk) paper with a low gloss ink' , producing a matt effect that understated the text and pictures and suggested a more newsy approach.

Was it worth all that trouble?

A 'blind tasting' of copies of *Vogue* and *Grazia* by a group of 20 fashion-conscious young women asked if they could find any physical difference between the two titles. The unanimous verdict was that *Grazia* felt 'more urgent'.

Not a bad response for a magazine that wanted so badly to be perceived as a weekly and not a monthly.

Online purchasers returning to books, paperbacks, magazines, vinyl, CDs and DVDs declare they have come to value the sense of possession, of owning a physical representation of the things that they enjoy instead of merely looking at a screen.

This was demonstrated at the Royal Wedding of Prince William and Kate Middleton when the whole nation watched, entranced by the spectacular intimacy of modern-day TV coverage – cameras seemingly everywhere, zooming from aerial shots of the whole scene to close-ups of the wedding ring finger, making viewers at home feel they were having a better view than the most distinguished members of the congregation.

Coverage went on around the clock, from the breakfast-time build-up to the happy couple's escape from the Palace by sports car. Replays of the highlights went on until midnight. Most people went to bed that Saturday night convinced that, yes, they really had been there.

So why did 1.4 million of them rush out next day to grab the Royal

Souvenir issue of *Hello!* magazine – in itself something of a media miracle in producing and distributing a 264-page issue in full colour in a matter of hours?

The answer is that in the cold light of the morning after, people realized they had only been spectators of the wedding through a window provided by the TV coverage; they had been staring at something going on far away OUTSIDE their home. The wedding souvenir brought the wedding INTO the house – literally to have and to hold.

The wedding now belonged to them, to scrutinize in detail and at leisure all that had been whizzed before their eyes.

Of course, the DVD would be available in due course, the whole thing could have been recorded on Sky+ and there was always the iPlayer. But trawling through hours of footage in search of those magic moments is much more labour-intensive than flicking through something sumptuous in its own right and sits comfortably on the lap, something to put away and keep in readiness for *Hello*'s souvenir issue of King William's coronation.

The physical quality of the magazine made it a desirable object. If they are to be possessed and enjoyed, all magazines must constantly try to look better, to feel better.

One editor of my distant acquaintance preferred practicality. His periodical, *Cage and Aviary Birds* was by far and away the most popular with keepers of all kinds of birds, from budgerigars to parrots and other tropical species. Although it was vastly profitable because as the brand leader it dominated the sector's advertising spend, the publication was in tabloid newspaper format and printed in black and white on poor-quality newsprint.

Yet he stubbornly resisted when urged to press his publishers to invest in the product; to go for a magazine format and insist on full colour on glossy paper to do full justice to the exotic plumage of his birds and to let his covers have more chance to pull in even more readers.

'My readers don't need colour on fancy paper to know what their birds look like,' he said. 'The tabloid size fits the bottom of the average bird cage and as cheap newsprint is very absorbent so each issue becomes a convenient liner to catch the droppings!'

But progress was not to be denied and currently *Cage and Aviary Birds* is truly a highly professional A4 magazine. Its covers feature some of the most colourful creatures ever to take wing and shine out from the news-stand.

A pity it can no longer serve its original purpose.

The souvenir issue of a Royal Wedding enables a distant spectacle to come into the home – an object to have and to hold

17 Putting It All Together

Story-telling is not the preserve of the fiction writer; it is the essence of journalism. And that means a story needs a carefully prepared plot if it is to hold the reader to the end

In fiction, the story springs from the imagination; in journalism it stems from reality and the challenge is to bring it convincingly to life. Words in themselves are inanimate. It is the way they are chosen and arranged that enables events to unfold before the reader's eyes, for characters to be seen to live and breathe, for information to be easily absorbed.

Arrangement is all and that is possible only when the necessary ingredients are fully identified and smoothly interwoven. Without an understanding of the VISA formula, the commissioning of a 1500-word feature is like a tailor being merely specified the height of the customer and the length of cloth. It needs to be fashioned to accommodate his knowledge of the basic elements of the human form to win admiration as a well-fitted suit.

If Location, Location, Location is the key to the art of interviewing, Construction, Construction, Construction is vital to the output of journalists working in text or online.

So how to achieve that?

1 From the first moments of preparation, mentally carry with you four pigeon-holes labelled Visuals, Information, Sounds and Action

2 Throughout research and in every interview, consciously, deliberately seek material that can be filed away in all four pigeon-holes. (These ingredients will not be delivered by chance)

3 Only contemplate the writing or production stage when you are satisfied that each pigeon-hole is well stocked (not necessarily with 25 per cent of each but well balanced according to the nature of the story)

4 Transcribe your notes into the four categories – placing them in those VISA pigeon holes

5 Pick-and-mix from those elements to arrive at a feature which demonstrates that words really can make pictures

In pre-digital days, I would type each anecdote on a separate sheet of paper, each nugget of information on a separate sheet, each piece of observation on a separate sheet and each quote on a separate sheet.

I would then sit on the floor, surrounded by four piles of paper, and use the carpet as a magnetic blackboard to achieve the necessary flow. Plucking sheets from each pile in turn and lining them up in front of me, switching their position back and forth. I might end up choosing that anecdote as possibly the most powerful opening, followed by that explanatory quote which led into that colourful piece of information which led to that physical description of the central character. And so on and so on. Never achieving the right mix straight away; often endlessly re-shuffling.

(A very similar process faces the journalist completing an online assignment, constantly permutating his raw material to achieve a storyboard in which his digital inserts of video, film, audio and graphics are most effectively positioned throughout the narrative. In whatever sequence they are deployed they should, as in print, be delivering a balanced blend of Visuals, Information, Sounds and Action.)

Within an overall mark that I awarded a student for a written exercise, I would give individual scores out of five for each of those categories. Scores of V4 – I2 – S5 – A2 might indicate a vivid description of the central character; insufficient hard information; excellent quotes; and a serious lack of anecdotes.

For an online feature, scores of V1 - I5 – S3 – A4 would suggest an unimaginative setting for the key interview; clever use of graphics; presenter's into-camera summing-up lacked authority; video fully captured the sense of confusion in the crowd.

My intention was to hammer home that a cake is only as good as its ingredients.

> The same principles of composition apply equally to print and online

Reporter who never used a notebook

Long before the digital revolution, a very similar mantra was observed by Gay Talese when the American came to fashioning his exhaustive research into the finished product. Never using a notebook, he had jotted his observations on pocket-sized cards – each one recording a separate interview, personal encounter, unexpected revelation or description of particular people, places and happenings.

These cards were marshalled into a series of 'scenes' which were then positioned within a storyboard deploying different elements of the feature picked out in red, blue and green ink, comprising a very personal form of colour-coding which no one else could faintly understand.

The earliest scribbled drafts – crammed with swooping arrows, soaring word balloons and hasty underlinings – suggested a child's graffiti. But the laborious end result was some of the finest features

> A series of scribbled 'scenes' enables a master journalist to display his craft

Discarding hard-earned material to meet the commissioned word-count is a difficult process and this is where the writer needs to take on the role of the hard-eyed sub-editor

ever written, with a truly scenic flow from beginning to end.

Talese's expenses also became legendary in the course of the 32 days he spent tracking the jet-set life of Frank Sinatra to produce a 15,000-word article. Such extravagance of money, time and space is out of the question in our more straitened times but whatever the budgetary and deadline constraints the diligent researcher will still almost certainly accumulate more material than the commissioned word-count can accommodate.

Just as Talese must have had to discard scores and scores of his jotting cards to get down to even 15,000 words, so must a feature writer not be afraid to discard often hard-won material which could not find a relevant placement.

This is where the writer turns dispassionate sub-editor.

If two or three incidents in my pile of anecdotes – however laboriously unearthed – turned out to illustrate the same element of the story, I would take a deep breath and cast aside all but the most telling.

Just as a CV should be ruthlessly purged to meet only the specific needs of the prospective employer, so I came to learn that blocks of solid information – however much of general interest – had to be consigned to my waste pile if not specifically meeting the demands and expectations of my target reader.

I found that description, however important in bringing colour, atmosphere and movement to the feature, needs to be carefully measured. Too much description is like applying too many layers of paint to a canvas and needlessly obscures the picture you want the reader to see.

Avoid quotes that ramble

Direct quotes should be kept to conversational length. People who are allowed to talk at great length are boring in the written word as well as in speech. Don't hesitate to take the sub-editor's cleaver to any passages of speech that tend to ramble.

Knowing what to cut, what to reject, is every bit as important as knowing what to put in.

Even when my final choice stretched in a line across the carpet I would often transpose whole blocks to and fro within the sequence to ensure the flow was as smooth as possible, that the four ingredients were kept in balance.

That ponderous process is not necessary in the computer age but the thought process should be the same. Create four separate folders and summon their various ingredients to the screen in turn, switching back and forth, mixing and matching until you achieve the ideal blend, not only within individual passages but throughout the piece overall. Much less labour-intensive than in typewriter days – so there is all the more reason not to stint the number of permutations in search of that end.

The best features do not come out in print or on screen the same way the raw material went into the notebook or recorder. The most telling material has to be extricated and assembled.

Time and again as a university lecturer, I was able to demonstrate how a student's submitted feature could be vastly improved without changing a single word – by merely rearranging the content in a more effective sequence.

The ultimate test when a feature is set for completion is for the writer to imagine it as a whole and then mentally distinguish each paragraph with one of the four Hallmarks that make up the VISA formula. If that exercise suggests an attractively varied pattern in the mind the chances are that the feature will delight the eyes of your readers as the words on page or screen are brought most immediately to life.

That's what story-telling is all about – whatever the subject or the mood, the manner of the telling should be enjoyable.

Always remember the trilogy of feature writing:

To Inform

To Educate

To Entertain

An attractive pattern formed by Hallmarks makes for a well-balanced piece of journalism

Index